MOUNTAIN BIKING IN BOISE

By Stephen Stuebner

First printing: *Mountain Biking in the Boise Front,* December 1994
Second printing: *Mountain Biking in the Boise Front,* June 1995
Third printing: *Mountain Biking in Boise,* November 1997
Fourth printing: *Mountain Biking in Boise,* October 2002

ACKNOWLEDGMENTS

I want to express special thanks to the landowners who granted temporary permission for trails on private land in the book, and thank them for granting easements to the Ridge to Rivers Trail Program. Thanks toTim Breuer, Ridge to Rivers trail coordinator, Donna Griffin, director of Ada Parks and Waterways, and Jim Hall, director of the Boise Parks and Recreation Department for their leadership in caring for Boise foothills trails and the Boise River Greenbelt. Special thanks to Jan Sutter, who developed many new maps for this book. And I wish to thank Marianne Nelson for modeling for the front cover on a frosty evening.

CREDITS:

Cover design: Sally Stevens
Computer mapping: Rick Gerrard, Jan Sutter
Illustrations: Patrick Davis
Photographs: All photos by the author, unless credits indicate otherwise.

On the cover: Marianne Nelson takes an evening cruise on the northern ti
of Table Rock. *Cover photo by Glenn Oakley.*

THE RIDES

BEGINNER

INTERMEDIATE

ADVANCED/EXPERT

PERSONAL FAVORITES

Mark Lisk rides up Hulls Gulch.

The Rides*

1. Boise River Greenbelt
2. Red Fox-Owl's Roost
3. Mores Mountain Loops
4. Military Reserve Beginner Loop
5. Oregon Trail Easy Loop
6. Tour of Pearl
7. Redtail Ridge Loop Loop
8. 36th Street-Harrison Hollow
9. Corrals-Trail #1 Loop
10. Banzai to Boise
11. Red Fox-Crestline-Red Cliffs
12. Military Reserve Tough Loop
13. Crestline-Hulls Gulch Loop
14. Shane's Trail
15. Table Rock Loops
16. Oregon Trail-Bonneville Point
17. Corrals-Bob's Loop
18. Scott's-8th Street-Hard Guy
19. Tour de Bogus Basin
20. Tour de Bogus II

21. Tour de Bogus III
22. Hard Guy-Dry Creek Loop
23. Crestline-Sidewinder-Trail #4
24. Crooked Summit-Pines Loop
25. 8th Street-Scott's-Corrals Loop
26. Three Bears Loop
27. Trails #4-#5-#6 Ridge Rider
28. Rocky Canyon-Trail #7 Loop
29. Rocky Canyon Right-Side Loop
30. Over the Top of Shaw Mountain
31. Squaw Creek Loops
32. Ken's Favorite Foothills Ride
33. Foothills on the Rocks
34. BOMB Squad Bruiser
35. Chris's Favorite Lunch Ride
36. Stuebie's Death March
37. Tom's Favorite Singletrack
38. Tom's 3-Hour Tour
39. Back of Beyond 8-Hour Tour
40. Ride to Mark's Cabin

*Match ride number with
master map on right.

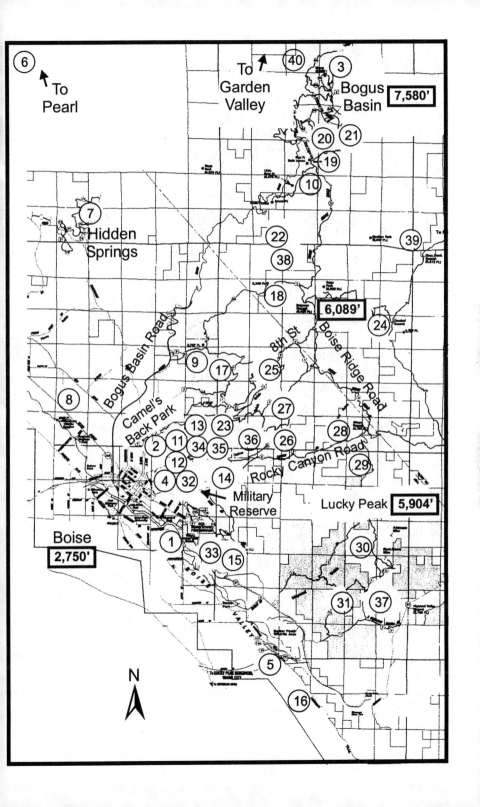

DISCLAIMER

WARNING: **MOUNTAIN BIKING INVOLVES A NUMBER OF UNAVOIDABLE RISKS THAT MAY CAUSE SERIOUS INJURY OR DEATH. THESE RISKS INCLUDE FLYING OFF YOUR BIKE AT INOPPORTUNE MOMENTS, MECHANICAL BREAKDOWNS, AND GETTING LOST. ANYONE WHO PURCHASES THIS BOOK ASSUMES ALL RISK AND RESPONSIBILITY FOR THEIR OWN SAFETY AND WELFARE.**

The author has attempted to provide an accurate description of each route in this guidebook. However, a route listed in this book may or may not be safe for anyone to ride at any given time. Routes vary in difficulty, and cyclists' abilities vary according to their experience and conditioning. Trails may change or deteriorate due to cataclysmic environmental or climatic events, new housing developments, logging, mining, wildfires, road-building or other circumstances beyond the author's control.

The trail descriptions and other information in this book are designed to help cyclists find new places to ride and equip cyclists with the necessary information about what to bring on a ride and how to prepare for it. Along with the information provided in this book, cyclists should carry topographic maps for the area in which they are riding before embarking on the ride. The time required to complete a ride is listed as a range, and it is approximate, depending on cyclists' experience and conditioning.

Some expert routes in this book are long, difficult rides that involve lengthy first-gear climbs for hours at a time. These rides could become a nightmare for beginning and intermediate cyclists. Intermediates and beginners who attempt an expert ride do so at their own risk. Never embark on an expert ride late in the day — you could break down, get caught by darkness, and spend a nasty cold night out in the woods.

Before you embark on a ride, tell someone where you are going and leave them a map of the trail. If you get lost, the Ada County Mountain Search and Rescue Team recommends that you stay put, build a fire and wait for help. To reach search and rescue in Ada County, call 911 or 846-7610. For other counties, call the sheriff's office for the county in which the person is lost.

Know your limitations and use common sense. It's better to give up on a ride than spend an uncomfortable night in the woods. Be alert, ride under control and always wear a helmet.

A FEW TIPS ON...

MOUNTAIN BIKE MANNERS

REMEMBER, ALL MOUNTAIN BIKERS WILL BE JUDGED BY YOUR CONDUCT...

Let's face it. The future of mountain biking is directly related to our conduct — our impact on trails and our relations with other trail users. It's called backcountry ethics.

Now comes the question, (how can we put this gently?) Do you know about backcountry ethics? Or as <u>Mountain Bike Action</u> editors put it, "Are you an "off-road idiot?" "Are you a "bicycling bonehead?" or "Are you a toxic trail user?"

No way! you might reply. "I'm not like all those yee-hah, subhumanoid adrenaline sniffers that *Geraldo* and *60 Minutes* feature in their Two-Wheeled Terrors' videos. Those legless bi-valves don't deserve to live, much less call themselves mountain bikers!"

OK. Let's not get into the blame game. But before you take off on your next mountain bike ride, read about mountain biking's biggest enemies — easily avoidable behavior that has led to trail closures in more populated areas — and learn how to set a positive example for your sport. It doesn't matter if you've been a bicycling bonehead before; no one will ever know. Just learn how to do it right.

Meet your enemies, as described by <u>Mountain Bike Action</u> editor Richard Cunningham, with subnotes by the author:

ENEMY NO. 1: MISTER CONTROL (AKA MR. SPEEDBALL)

"Mr. Control rides at top speed everywhere, slowing only slightly to pass other trail users. He thinks that uttering a sharp "On your left!" as he blows by is a polite exchange of goodwill. Hikers or other cyclists have told him that he's causing others to freak out and that it would be best if he stopped or slowed to walking speed to let others pass quietly. Mr. Control blows 'em off.... Mr. Control is a mental case."

Bottom line: Ride under control and be prepared to slow down for ALL trail users coming up the trail. Bend over backwards to be polite and show fellow trail users that mountain bikers can, indeed, show respect for other folks and share the trail.

Remember: One bad encounter with a hiker, jogger or equestrian will leave a *permanent* negative impression about all mountain bikers.

ENEMY NO. 2: REAR BRAKE RODNEY

"Rear Brake Rodney is the most common backcountry bonehead. Forsaking the laws of physics, Rodney refuses to use his front brake. This dude is the skid kid. Rod refuses to believe that most of the weight of his bike transfers to the front wheel under braking, making his rear stopper ineffective. Instead, Rodney the Ridiculous excavates the trail surface, locking up his rear wheel, skidding into every curve and carving a rut down the center of downhill singletracks....

"The most lame excuse is that locking the rear end up is a faster or more controllable way to ride.... Mastering the front brake is a fat-tire essential. Locking up the brakes is uncool on singletracks. Besides the fact that it digs up the trail, Rear Brake Rodney leaves ugly stripes that scream, "Follow this broken line to discover another out-of-control cyclist." The front brake is the most important tool for technical riding, especially on

Rear-Brake Rodney tears up the trail.

steep downhills (ask any pro). Learn how to use it. (Rear Brake Rodney's prison sentence should be to adopt and maintain a single-track that his fellow skidders use. That'll cure him)."

Tip: When descending a steep trail, put about 65 percent of your braking power on your front brake lever, 35 percent on your back, and "feather" the back brake as you descend. It also helps to lower your seat and shift your butt over the back tire. "Feathering" the back brake means gripping the brake, and releasing it in rapid fashion. Try it: you'll notice that the skidding stops and you have much more control. If you've done all of the above and you're still skidding, the hill is too steep. Get off and walk.

Enemy No. 3: Predators in Paradise

"Twenty-odd fat-tire cyclists, decked out in team jerseys, racing flat out, side-by-side, is awesome in a closed race course. Put these predators in a local park on a peaceful afternoon and it's a recipe for hateful confrontation. Race training groups suffer from a subhuman pack mentality. If the front of the group burns past a couple of equestrians, invariably the rest will follow. Keeping everyone's speed down in sensitive areas is next to impossible."

The bottom line: Ride in small groups and *never* race on commonly used trails.

Enemy No. 4: Mr. Conveniently Handicapped

"No, this isn't the person who returns from a track meet and parks in a handi-

8

capped space to dash into the shopping mall for a latte. This dude is far worse, lower than gum on the floor of a subway station. Mr. Conveniently Handicapped is a local dude who rides illegally past every "No Bicycles" and "Trail Closed" sign in the surrounding parks. All of his friends, and most of the park rangers, have spoken to him about the regulations, but somehow Mr. Convenient thinks the rules are for someone else."

Bottom line: Please heed trail closure signs.

ENEMY NO. 5: VERNON THE VELO-SKIER

"Every Saturday Vernon and a handful of his buddies load up a couple pickup trucks with bikes and beer, then head to the local mountains for some serious downhill fun. They ride only one trail that used to be a popular hiking trail. One thing's for certain — there's absolutely no climbing involved. Vernon and his buds are Velo-Skiers. Once the caravan reaches the lower trailhead, someone shuttles the whole crew to the top. Vern and his buddies race each other to the bottom, then repeat their gravity game until dark-thirty or they run out of beer and baloney sandwiches. Vern and his buds rule this trail. What will happen if Vern and his buddies keep downhill skiing on the same trail? Authorities will close it to mountain bikes for good.

"Velo-skiing is cool; honing your downhill skills in a multi-use area isn't. There is a time and place for screamin' fast descents. Now that most ski areas are open for cycling during the summer, there is no reason to terrorize the local parks. If you are too cheap to shell out $10 or $15 for a lift ticket, downhill in motorcycle areas where other users are expecting high-speed encounters."

ENEMY NO. 6: ADAM & EVE'S PALSY

"Adam and Eve live in the mountains, surrounded by miles of roads and single-tracks. Most mountain bikers would think their local trails were heaven. Unfortunately, life at high altitude must have affected their brains. For some reason, they only ride in wilderness areas that are strictly off-limits to bicycles (or any other mechanical devices, for that matter).... Wilderness areas are hallowed ground among the most powerful environmental groups; stay out of them! Conversely, the fact that there are places that people can go to escape bicycles and other devices gives us a strong bargaining chip to win access to the remaining backcountry. Don't blow it for the rest of us. Stay away from the forbidden fruit."

ENEMY NO. 7: LEWIS & CLARK

"These dudes are dangerous dreamers. Armed with a brain the size of a pinhead, these two brothers boast knowledge of every park within 20 miles. In fact, they are self-appointed trail blazers who have pioneered at least half of the nearby single-tracks. Trouble is, nobody asked these gophers to start digging. Their "trails" are steep, hard to maintain and don't go anywhere in particular.... Like most wannabe trail-breakers, Lewis and Clark simply rode across any interesting space between two roads. Others followed their tracks until a new trail was born."

This is a bad deal for everyone. Before you self-appoint yourself to cut a new trail, talk to the landowner first. Their likely response will be: Don't do it. We've got enough trouble maintaining the trails we have.

Enemy No. 8: City Slackers

"These folks are easy to spot. They own pretty nice bikes and dress up in the type of mountain bike gear that the models wear on Jeep TV commercials.... Are you a slacker? Your only salvation is to get down to a good fat-tire bike store, hook up with a couple of authentic mountain bikers, then go out and experience the real McCoy."

Enemy No. 9: Calvin Cutter

"Redwood remora, singletrack slime, trail tick, berm bait ... no trailside insult is rude enough to describe Calvin the Switchback Cutter. ... Why is it so important for somebody to shorten their journey by five or 10 feet in the middle of the woods? It sounds petty, doesn't it? Yet, hikers, cyclists and equestrians are all guilty of destroying switchbacks by shortcutting the last few steps."

Enemy No. 10: Barbara Badger

"Barbara the Badger has been mountain biking for a long time. She has done her share of trail maintenance, worked to mend fences with local mountain bike factions and gets in a few races each year. In the past she has been extremely courteous, but lately, one too many confrontations with hateful hikers has made her bitter.

"As a result, Barbara and her cycling partners have given up any pretense of being nice to hikers. Now, instead of a casual trailside greeting, she manages a tight-lipped smile. Rather than stopping to allow others to pass by easily, she slows to an acceptable pace and goes on her merry way. Barbara still cares about joint trail use, but she has lost faith in the system and has begun to give up trying to be nice at all.

"Giving up is the worst enemy mountain bikers have to fight. Don't waste your good nature upon some backcountry sourpuss. If someone gives you grief, smile, give 'em a quick, "See ya later," then leave. Peer pressure and good faith are the most powerful tools we have to overcome ignorance."

INTRODUCTION

Welcome to one of the best and most accessible urban-backcountry trail systems in America. We are privileged to have more than 80 miles of singletrack and jeep trails right outside the back door of Boise, Idaho's capital city, and nearly 20 miles of paved Greenbelt pathways that run alongside the Boise River through a series of beautiful public parks. For people who want to discover the true sport of mountain biking, the steep-rising, angular mountains north of Boise feature a treasure chest of mountain biking adventures — tons of singletrack and primitive two-track trails, lots of technical climbs, huge descents, and many links from one ridge to the next.

It's just simply heaps of huge fun for mountain bikers. And it's all there for the taking. All you need is a mountain bike and the urge to explore.

Many of the trails in this book are part of the Ridge to Rivers Trail System, an 80-mile network of linked mountain and urban trails -- from an elevation of 7,580 feet at the top of Bogus Basin Ski Area, to the Boise River Greenbelt, nearly 5,000 feet below, and many points in between. This book includes all of the best trails in the Ridge to Rivers Trail network, plus a number of other trails in the Boise area. This book complements the Ridge to Rivers map by providing details about foothills trails, such as difficulty, length, vertical gain, directions, etc. This book also contains all of the new trails that volunteers from the Southwest Idaho Mountain Biking Association (SWIMBA) built in cooperation with government agencies, Boise area businesses including REI, trail-friendly landowners, the BLM, and Tim Breuer, the Ridge to Rivers trail coordinator.

This fourth edition of *Mountain Biking in Boise* contains a totally new, exciting element. Considering that many riders already know the trail system, I figured folks might enjoy hearing from avid riders about their favorite rides. Several of the rides fall into the epic category. Check out these personal favorites and spice up your mountain bike repertoire.

Here in 2002, despite the major boom we've seen in residential, commercial and industrial development in the Boise Valley over the last 15 years, it's pretty amazing to realize that we've seen a *net gain* in trail mileage in the foothills and along the Greenbelt. A few natural disasters have reshaped the land, such as the 15,300-acre wildfire in August 1996, and a flash flood in September 1997, which brought major engineering solutions (terracing, new flood-control dams and structures). But the trail system has survived; trails have been rerouted to ensure there is no net loss to the trail system.

One major reason we have so many trails to enjoy in the Boise area is because private landowners have been especially generous in providing temporary or permanent easements for public trails. In addition, the Boise City Council and the Ada County Commission have required developers to provide links to public trails adjacent to new developments. Many developers have integrated new Greenbelt pathways into housing projects. All of these efforts, combined with new trails built by volunteers, have resulted in the wonderful trail system we enjoy today.

Still, please be aware that trail network in the Boise foothills and along the Oregon Trail overlies a mish-mash of land ownership, including a ton of private land. There is a critical gap of private land in between city parks at the base of the foothills and BLM and U.S. Forest Service land in the upper foothills. That's why Boise Mayor Brent Coles called on city residents to support a $10 million levy to purchase open space, wildlife easements and trail easements in the foothills. Coles led an impressive political coalition in May 2001 to win a levy election by a 60 percent vote. Key players in that coalition included the Idaho Conservation League, SWIMBA, neighborhood associations, foothills recreationists, city parks board members, artist Carl Rowe and foothills lovers in general. Now the Boise Parks and Recreation Department is working with The Trust for Public Lands and The Nature Conservancy to secure as much private property as possible, in strategic locations, to preserve and enhance the trail system, protect open space for wildlife and the environment, and preserve the city's trademark backdrop. The $10 million levy will ensure that the acquisition of open space will be a high priority in the foothills for years to come.

It's been an exciting adventure to seek out and catalogue all of the trails in this book — from the Boise Foothills, to Bogus Basin, to the Oregon Trail, and points far beyond the Boise Ridge toward Idaho City and Garden Valley. Many mountain bikers have their favorite places to ride, but I encourage cyclists to spread out as much as possible and take the initiative to try new trails. See if you can't tackle all the trails in this book in a single riding season. If you can accomplish that, you'll be a strong expert by the end of the summer.

It's always a rewarding experience to ride a new trail, see some new country-side, cruise down a draw or a ridge spine that you haven't toured before. Maybe you'll see a golden eagle swoop down and nail a jackrabbit just 50 feet away. Maybe you'll see a bird nest, a covey of quail, catch a glimpse of a fox, a coyote, a soaring red-tailed hawk or a herd of deer. Enjoy!

SHOW RESPECT FOR THE LAND, FELLOW TRAIL USERS

Remember, the conduct of all mountain bikers will determine our future. The three most important things for mountain bikers to remember is to:

■Practice soft-cycling techniques — take pride in leaving little to no trace on the trail.

■Show respect and be courteous to other trail users, such as hikers, joggers, equestrians, motorcyclists, ATVs and others. Yield right of way to pedestrians at all times, and to uphill mountain bikers.

■Show respect for private land — obey no trespassing signs, pick up garbage, close gates, etc.

The key cornerstone of trail ethics in Idaho is that people are friendly and courteous. Next time you see someone approaching on the trail, pause to say hello and yield right of way. To show courtesy and respect for hikers, joggers, horseback riders and motorcyclists is a progressive attitude that will ensure a long future for all of us.

BIKE MAINTENANCE
Tool Kits and Repairs

Anyone who ventures into the backcountry for a mountain biking adventure should carry a basic tool kit, patch kit and hand pump to cope with flat tires and other common breakdowns. Even Greenbelt riders will be glad to have a pump and patch kit with them if they get a flat, especially if they ride to Lucky Peak.

I recommend carrying a few extra tools in your vehicle if you happen to drive to a trailhead, and bringing along the key essentials on the ride itself.

RECOMMENDED BARE-ESSENTIAL TOOL KIT FOR YOUR BIKE:*

Hand pump   Allen wrenches
Extra slime tube   Patch kit
Tire irons   Spoke wrench
Chain breaker   Chain lube

*Many multipurpose tools, like the "Cool Tool," provide allen wrenches, a chain-breaking tool, crescent wrench, pliers, and other items in one tool.

RECOMMENDED TOOL KIT FOR YOUR VEHICLE:

Hand pump (preferably an upright, powerful one)
Spokes   Grease rags
Extra patch kit   Freewheel remover
Brake cables   Extra bearings
Derailleur cables   Screwdrivers
Extra chain   Crescent wrench

RECOMMENDED SAFETY GEAR:

Rain gear   First-aid kit
Compass or GPS unit   Lighter or matches
Space blanket   Topographic map

To make your mountain bike outings more pleasurable, keep your bike in good running condition, either through preventative maintenance at home or at a bike shop. Keeping your bike clean, adjusting cables, keeping the rims true, replacing bearings and periodically replacing a worn, stretched-out chain will help avoid major breakdowns on the trail.

Tips for Coping with Breakdowns

Problem: Broken rear derailleur
Solution: Create a one-speed with your chain tool
Open up a chainlink with the chain tool, shorten the chain and bypass the non-functional rear derailleur. Put your chain on the middle chain ring in the front and in the middle ring of your rear sprocket. This creates a one-speed bike that you'll be able to ride home.

Problem: Frequent flat tires due to thorns or "goat heads"
Solution: Slime/new tube
Trails in the drier parts of Idaho often contain goat heads, a noxious plant that spreads seeds with nail-like spikes. In an especially unlucky situation, you can fly off the trail and end up with 20 punctures in your tire tube. There are three ways to combat this problem: 1) Install slime or self-sealing tubes inside your tire; 2) Carry a spare tube; 3) Carry a patch kit.

Problem: You get a flat, and your friend's pump (the only one you have with you) works only for presta valves.
Solution: Carry a valve adapter in your tool kit so you can borrow someone's pump regardless of whether it works for presta or schrader valves. Or, carry your own pump and you won't have to depend on someone else to bail you out. Some pumps have reversible valve fittings. If you don't like presta valves, have your local bike shop drill bigger holes in your rim that fit schrader valves.

Do I Really Need a Helmet?

Most definitely. There's a number of reasons why. Here's four:
1. It's cheap life insurance.
2. It's the smart thing to do.
3. Experienced riders won't immediately peg you as a rookie.
4. If you fly over your handlebars, your helmet will soften the blow to your brain.

Medical research shows conclusively that wearing a hard-shell helmet reduces the risk of head and brain injury in the event of a crash. Consider this:

■Between 1993 and 1996, 12 people in Idaho were killed in bicycle-related crashes and 1,266 were involved in bicycle-automobile collisions. Fewer than 10 percent of the riders involved in collisions were wearing a helmet, according to the Idaho Department of Transportation.

■A medical study of mountain bike accidents in the Seattle area showed that most mountain bikers (80 percent) wore helmets, and that helmets reduced the risk of head injury by 85 percent, and the risk of brain injury by 88 percent.

Spinning Up the Mountain

It's true: riding uphill on a mountain bike is difficult and challenging, especially in *real* mountains, eh? It makes your heart race, it makes your thighs burn, it makes you sweat, and very often, it hurts.

However, there's a method to the madness. It's called Zen and the Art of Climbing Hills. To master the basic technique of hill-climbing requires the correct mental attitude, learning how to gear down quickly, deft adjustments in body position, preserving your strength on long rides and the broad use of gears.

First, even if you find hills intimidating, you've got to develop the right mental attitude about hill climbing. Why did you buy a mountain bike? To ride in the mountains, of course. You don't want to be a spectator, you want to be a participant. It's time to get those shiny new bike tights dirty and show your friends and neighbors that you're a real stud or a true luscious mountain babe. You dream of getting in good enough shape to climb roads and trails to a mountain peak where you can see for 100 miles in all directions. You yearn to to keep up with your buffed friends, and even better, to have a pair of sleek, muscle-toned legs to show off at a local bar after the ride.

Well, just like anything else, you've got to pay your dues. But hey, the good news is that a mountain bike was built especially for climbing. Unlike the one-speed bike you rode as a kid, mountain bikes have a huge range of gears, now, typically 27 speeds. That means you should be able to climb most any dirt road in the mountains. It's just a matter of how fast you go, and how long your legs can handle the grade before you get pooped.

The most important thing to remember when riding hills is the higher you climb, the longer you'll be able to scream downhill and revel in one gigantic head rush. Aha! That's why gonzo mountain bikers love to climb so much -- they're always seeking a big downhill rush.

OK, now you're ready to build up a sweat, burn some calories and get in shape. Start by riding a continuous, predictable grade, like Table Rock Road, Cartwright Road, 8th Street or Rocky Canyon Road to build some endurance.

Proper Gear Selection Is Essential

Storm up the mountain! Carry as much momentum as you can from the flats or a downhill section into the climb. Stay in a big gear until you start feeling the hill in your legs, then gear down slowly, one or two gears at a time until you reach the comfort zone. If you face an abrupt, steep climb after a steep downhill, however, you'll have to drop into an easy gear right as the steep climb begins. This takes anticipation, practice and experience to know what gears you can push on a particular grade. If in doubt, drop into 1st or 2nd gear.

Correct body position is another key part of climbing hills to prevent the rear tire from spinning out. First, as tempting as it might be to stand up on steep hills, stay in the saddle. It increases the weight over your back tire, and thus, increases traction. If the hill is steep enough that the front wheel starts popping up off the ground, slide forward a little in the saddle. On REALLY STEEP spots with good traction, you may need to stand on the pedals and lean over the handlebars to keep the front wheel on the ground. However, it's best to stay seated as much as possible because many trails will be too loose to allow standing on the pedals. You'll spin out, waste energy and stop dead in your tracks.

MORE CLIMBING TIPS:

- Relax -- rarely will you need a death grip on the handle bars.
- Install cleated pedals for efficient riding.
- Practice proper breathing technique. When you find yourself breathing hard, take very deep breaths and then, purse your lips and exhale slowly. This technique helps pump more oxygen into your body and gives you more climbing and staying power.
- Make sure your seat is adjusted properly for maximum power (your knees should be slightly bent at full extension).
- Spin easy gears to avoid burning up all your energy in the first hill; as you get in better shape, try to push bigger gears. But be careful! Pushing big gears on steep hills may lead to a myriad of injuries or muscle cramps.
- Concentrate when riding on singletrack trails; a small obstacle such as a bush, tree root or rock may force you off your bike. In order to avoid this, look ahead for obstacles.
- Install bar-ends on your handlebars to help keep weight over the front wheel when climbing steep hills and allow more efficient use of upper body strength.
- Reduce tire pressure slightly for better traction on loose dirt; however, be sure to follow the tire pressure guidelines for minimum and maximum inflation (it's etched on the side of the tire).
- Always drink plenty of water — it enhances endurance, and prevents dehydration and cramps.
- Carry extra food, such as energy bars or trail mix, in case you need more fuel after a long climb. Otherwise, you might "bonk" (run out of fuel, so to speak).

Riding Down the Mountain

To fully enjoy a thrilling and safe descent on a mountain bike, it's important to learn a few braking and body-positioning techniques to avoid major wipeouts, broken bones, and, well, serious bodily harm.

Before flying down a mountain trail totally out of control, take the time to master a few basic skills. Begin by learning the power of your front brake, and realize that you need to use BOTH your front and back brakes for maximum control. In general, when you approach a hill, shift your weight to your feet, and place your pedals in parallel fashion at the 9 o'clock and 3 o'clock position. Transfer your body weight toward the rear of your seat. Stand on your pedals for balance, keeping your butt an inch or two off the saddle. Keep at least one finger on each brake lever, for quick braking action, as necessary. It's also a good idea to place your chain in the middle or large ring on downhill sections to keep your chain taut and prevent a loose chain from clanging against your spokes and frame. Keep your legs and arms bent, and relax — let your bike shocks and your arms and legs absorb the shock.

As you're gliding down the trail, it's important to pay extra attention to prevent your back tire from skidding, which causes erosion, and causes you to lose control. The best way to avoid skidding is to "feather" your back brake by pulling on the lever, releasing it, and pulling on it again. You'll be amazed. The technique really works!

A front shock on a mountain bike greatly reduces the blunt impacts on your arms and wrists. We recommend one for active riders. Rear shocks provide the biggest advantage when riding downhill. They soften the blows as you glide over the top of rocks and roots, enabling you to go even faster. Riding with a rear shock makes riding downhill much smoother, almost like skiing.

On extremely steep descents – situations in which you may have to shift your butt over the top of your back tire (known as the hemorrhoid-polishing position) -- it's a good idea to lower your seat post a few inches. Then, it will be easier to shift your body behind the seat without banging certain very delicate body parts.

More Downhill Tips

■When encountering deep sand, rocks and ruts, you may feel as if you're losing control of your front wheel. The solution: Release the brakes and coast through the obstacle(s). Keep your weight toward the back. Once you've gained control again, apply the brakes again as necessary.

■Carry speed through rocky or sandy areas -- it helps keep your balance.

■As the trail gets steeper, shift your weight farther to the rear of the bike.

■Learn to bunny-hop or wheelie over rocks and other obstacles. The key is to lift up with your pedals and arms prior to the obstacle and pre-jump it. This is a very effective technique that can be practiced in your driveway. Place a 2x4 on the driveway, and practice jumping it without striking the wood.

INTERPRETIVE INFORMATION

GEOLOGY, HISTORY, FLOODS, FIRES, FAUNA...

Geology: The Boise Front is a geologic mish-mash of granitic rock, basalt lava flows and large deposits of sedimentary rock, i.e., sand and sandstone. The southern-most lobe of the Idaho Batholith, a largely homogenous hunk of granite that underpins much of central Idaho, dips into the Boise Front. Off to the side of many trails, you will see granite spires and outcroppings — the first visible hints of the batholith. Farther to the east, on the lower reaches of Shaw Mountain, Columbia basalt flows form the crown around the edges of aptly named Table Rock. The walls of the "black cliffs," as rock climbers refer to the basalt walls bordering the Boise River near Diversion Dam, also are remnants of oozing lava flows.

The quarry on the east flank of Table Rock was first developed in 1877 to tap into a sandstone deposit for building the old state penitentiary and a few structures in downtown Boise. Inmates at the state pen were required to work in the quarry. They were called the "Hill Gang." Blocks of sandstone were lowered with a horse-drawn cart. The quarry was still in use in 2002 by a private mining company.

Native Americans: Shoshone Indians occupied the Boise Valley, as well as many other mountain valleys across southern Idaho, for several thousand years prior to white settlement. The Shoshone people were hunters and gatherers. They subsisted on salmon (the river ran thick with salmon in those days, prior to the dams that killed off the ocean-going runs), camas, bitterroot and other plants and roots, elk and deer. After horses of Spanish origin were traded to the tribes in the 1700s, Indians became more mobile. The Boise Valley became a trading center and a gathering place for ceremonial dances during the salmon runs in August and September. The gathering became known as the "Sheewoki Fair." The Northern Paiute, Umatilla, Cayuse, Nez Perce, Cheyenne, Arapaho and Crow tribes joined the Shoshone in the festivities, according to the late Merle Wells, an Idaho historian. The Shoshone were driven out of the area in the 1860s after a fort was established at Fort Boise and the mining boom began in the Idaho City area.

Trappers: The first party of fur trappers arrived in the Boise Valley in the fall of 1811, led by Donald Mackenzie, who worked for the Pacific Fur Co. at the time. French-Canadian trappers are credited with naming the cottonwood-lined Boise River "bois," meaning "wooded" in French. The Boise River Basin and the Payette River Basin were reportedly rich in beaver supplies. A trading center was developed at the mouth of the Boise River near present-day Parma in the mid-1830s. Francois Payette, a French-Canadian trapper for whom the Payette River is named, was master of Fort Boise for nearly a decade.

Oregon Trail: In the 1840s, the westward movement of pioneers commenced on the Oregon Trail and other long-distance trails. It's still possible to see the route taken by Oregon Trail emigrants from Bonneville Point, a high knob above Lucky

Peak Reservoir, down the grade on the upper rim overlooking the Boise River. The Kelton Ramp, located on a bluff south of Surprise Valley, was one of the routes that emigrants used to drop into the valley from the upper rim. Historical reports indicate that about 300,000 people traveled on the Oregon Trail between the early 1840s and the 1860s.

Fort Boise was established in what would become the township of Boise on July 4, 1863 by Major Pinckney Lugenbeel of the U.S. Army. Lugenbeel selected the site of what is now Military Reserve in east Boise. The city of Boise was established three days afterward on July 7. The fort was constructed of wood, fetched from the vicinity of Shaw Mountain. A toll road used to run up Cotton-wood Creek from the Fort Boise site, but it has been relocated since private property blocks the historic route.

The toll road was one of the first dirt roads carved into the Boise foothills to give gold miners access over the mountains to the Boise Basin, Grimes Creek and the Idaho City area. The toll road was first opened for wagon travel in 1864, two years after George Grimes made the first gold strike in the Boise Basin. Early squatters gained property rights along the road, including a man named Hugh Clawson. Near the site of where Rocky Canyon Road meets Orchard Gulch (Trail #7 trailhead, about 5 miles up the road, on the north side), Clawson collected a toll ranging from $1 to $10 per vehicle, according to Walter M. Williams, an Idaho Statesman writer. Williams wrote that folks like Clawson told travelers, "Mister, the road is free, but the gate is mine. It will cost you something to swing it." Hundreds of prospectors and others depended on the toll road as the gold boom lasted for more than 40 years, although the first decade or so was the most productive.

Before the old toll road was built, the Cottonwood Creek draw was probably an old Indian trail, Williams said. He described the grade as a "Coney Island roller coaster."

Foothills mines: During the gold boom in the 1800s, several mines were developed in upper Rocky Canyon, according to the Wells, in his book Gold Camps and Silver Cities. The remains of several mines can still be seen up Orchard Gulch, Five-Mile Creek and on the east slope of Lucky Peak, the Black Hornet mines. Of these, the Black Hornet was the most productive. A single gold nugget worth $69.95 was discovered at the Black Hornet, which immediately attracted investors. By 1896, the mines had netted about $30,000 worth of gold, and later on, a total of $400,000 had rolled in.

Early trails: Eighth Street was built by the military in the late 1890s to access a new wood supply on the Boise Ridge. The toll road, and the South Contour Road on Shaw Mountain provided access to wood. The original route and grade of 8th Street has been changed. In places, the old road grade can be detected as you're riding up 8th Street.

Bogus Basin Road was first developed as a dirt road in the late 1930s. The ski area first opened for business in the early 1940s. It's one of the oldest ski areas in Idaho, along with Sun Valley.

Other jeep trails and singletrack trails in the foothills have evolved over time from use by the Shoshone Indians, trappers, miners, sheep and cattle, ranchers, and more recently, modern-day recreationists.

Mountain biking first began -- in its most primitive sense -- in the Boise Front when people like Merle Wells, his brother, Don, and friend Robert Romig, used to push their one-speed Schwinn bicycles up 8th Street or Bogus Basin Road in the 1930s, and then ride downhill on the Ridge Road to Rocky Canyon Road and back to town. It's possible, of course, that others may have preceded Wells and his friends, but how many young people would have had the gumption and strength to push a bike 3,000 vertical feet uphill for eight miles, especially in those days?

Trails on Bearback Mountain, the name of the grassy knoll where trails criss-cross between 36th Street and Bogus Basin Road, were cut by livestock and people on the old Smith estate. The Franklin B. Smith homestead was established in 1863 near the location of 28th Street and Hill Road. Much of that estate has been developed by family members Richard B. Smith and his son, Geoff Smith.

For many years, the foothills were considered a "wasteland," a place where people dumped garbage and old cars. During the BLM's annual Tending the Foothills cleanup day on the first Saturday in May, volunteers have hauled old car bodies, refrigerators and washing machines out of Cottonwood Creek and Hulls Gulch, among other locations. Each year, new trail projects completed as part of Tending the Foothills have enhanced the trail system.

Fires, floods and mudslides: Because foothills soil consists of granite and sand, among other things, the land is highly erodible. During the summer, the foothills appear dry and baked in the sun. But during wet periods and spring snowmelt, the soil can erode and cause major cracks or gouges on roads, trails and on mountain sides. A dramatic illustration of this occurred in August 1959, when heavy rain fell on top of Shaw Mountain and other parts of the foothills. Earlier that month, a wildfire had charred 9,500 acres in the foothills, creating a situation ripe for disaster. When the hard rains came, they literally stripped the soil and vegetation off the mountains. Mud and water caked the

Natural Resources Conservation Service

A bulldozer clears mud and debris from the yard of an east Boise home in 1959.

streets of Boise. Cottonwood Creek rose from its typical late-summer trickle to a raging torrent. The peak velocity on Aug. 20, 1959, measured 3,000 cubic feet per second, a huge flow for a small creek. A short documentary film of the great flood, called the "Pot Boiled Over," is available from the Boise National Forest.

In response to the flood and watershed damage, a group of federal and state agencies built contour-terracing trenches and reseeded about 1,100 acres of land on the southwest face of Shaw Mountain. Today, the terraces still can be easily seen on the upper reaches of the mountain.

Of course, a similar combination of wildfire and flooding in the foothills in 1996 and 1997 resulted in even more ambitious and expensive engineering solutions.

It all started on Aug. 26, 1996, when someone was target shooting with tracer bullets (the kind that explode on impact) at the police department firing range in Military Reserve on a windy, 104-degree afternoon. One of the tracer bullets missed the target, and sparked a wildlife on the hillside behind the range, according to federal firefighting authorities. In minutes, the fire raced out of control and blew from east to west in the lower foothills, threatening hundreds of homes and people.

By nightfall, the worst of it was over. About 15,300 acres of land in the central core of the foothills was charred. Miraculously, only one home was destroyed. The fire consumed thousands of acres of wildlife habitat and the core of the foothills trail system, from portions of Shane's Trail on the east, to Bogus Basin Road on the west. The fire burned up trail bridges and erosion-control structures in Hulls Gulch, the Corrals Trail and Bob's Trail, leaving nothing but rebar sticking up like tombstones.

Ravi Miro Fry

Scorched earth in the Boise foothills after a 15,300-acre wildfire in August 1996. Eighth Street is the dirt road on the left. (Photo courtesy U.S. Forest Service)

Just two days after the fire ignited, the BLM's top managers reached out to the Boise National Forest, the Natural Resources Conservation Service (NRCS), the Idaho National Guard, Idaho Fish and Game, the city of Boise, Ada County, and key public interest groups (including SWIMBA) to develop a game plan for restoring the foothills. In a matter of two weeks, they put the plan into action. For a federal agency to move that rapidly on any kind of project is almost unheard of. The most impressive and important part of the restoration effort was that the BLM's leaders immediately reached out to the community for guidance and assistance, and took advantage of business and community support to get a huge amount of work accomplished before winter arrived with a roar in November.

By mid-September, a series of rehabilitation projects were scheduled every weekend to plant bitterbrush, install hay bales and erosion-control devices, remove fire-scorched signs, fencing and other equipment, and work on restoring and reopening 26 miles of trails. A total of 486 volunteers worked on these projects, as well as inmate crews from the Ada County jail and state penitentiary, donating 2,130 hours of labor. Local businesses provided food for volunteers every weekend. Idaho National Guard and U.S. Army crews swept the foothills for dangerous unexploded ordnance that had been shot into the foothills many years before. Law-enforcement teams worked to protect public safety and keep the public out of dangerous areas. The National Weather Service worked with the federal agencies to install new water gauges in strategic locations to help forewarn of possible floods and mud flows. Countless public meetings were held to inform Boise residents about the dangers of flooding, and an emergency readiness network was established -- all driven by fears that the 1959 mudflows might happen again.

The downside of the fast-track rehabilitation effort was that the NRCS, Boise National Forest and BLM leaders decided to immediately terrace the upper tier of the foothills near Trail #4 and 8th Street in the fall of 1996 with practically no public input or environmental analysis.

About $5 million was spent on check dams and other flood-control measures in the bottom of Crane Creek, Stewart Gulch, Cottonwood Creek and Hulls Gulch, which will protect homes downstream from flash floods.

On Sept. 11, 1997, a very short but heavy rainstorm in the upper portion of the foothills caused flash floods in Hulls Gulch and Crane Creek. The storm blew out all of the footbridges in upper Hulls Gulch. It also caused heavy boulder-rolling and erosion in the lower part of Bob's Trail. The flooding event reminded us that even a year after the fire, when lots of grass and vegetation had grown back, the soil in the foothills was still very unstable. It was kind of like watching geology in motion.

Birds and wildlife: As you ride the trails of the Boise Front, watch for birds and wildlife. A wide variety of songbirds are visible, depending on the time of year. A rich variety of birds of prey soar over the foothills, including bald eagles, red-tailed hawks, golden eagles, prairie falcons, American kestrels, Cooper's hawks, sharp-shinned hawks, turkey vultures and northern harriers. Raptor experts have been studying and counting birds of prey on top of Lucky Peak as part of a fall migration study. Researchers have discovered that many species of birds pass through the Boise Foothills prior to migrating south to Mexico and southern California. "The ridge acts as a natural funnel to southward-migrating birds," said Greg

John Watts

A bald eagle feeds on carrion in the Boise Foothills.

Kaltenecker, coordinator of the raptor migration project. "It is the southern-most timbered ridge extending into the plain, and it contains good habitats, which provide migrants with food, cover and roosting sites."

Many other forms of wildlife can be seen in the foothills. Watch for great-horned owls in the thick draws. Bald eagles can be seen soaring in the winter, but they typically roost along the Boise River. During the winter months, the Boise Foothills become a key winter range for more than 3,000 mule deer. Please observe the seasonal October-April closures in the Squaw Creek and Highland Valley areas to protect the deer. Ruffed and blue grouse will spook you when they flush from a draw. Quail are plentiful in creek-bottoms as

John Watts

Quail are commonly seen in foothills draws.

well. Other wildlife in the front include beaver, coyote, fox, badgers, marmots, skunks, rattlesnakes and bull snakes.

Rare plants: Three "rare" plants grow in the Boise Foothills: Mulford's milkvetch (*Astragalus mulfordiae*); Aase's onion (*allium aaseae*); and Slick-spot peppergrass (*Lepidium papilliferum*). All three are listed as a "species of special concern," one tier below a proposal for full protection under the Endangered Species Act. Under this management classification, the BLM's wildlife biologists have forged a conservation agreement with the city of Boise and Ada County in hopes of protecting the remaining populations of these rare plants. Under federal law, however, private landowners are not required to inventory their land for rare plants or protect them, according to the BLM.

MOUNTAIN BIKING AT NIGHT

There's something eerie and mysterious about the darkness of night. Fear of the unknown. Deep quiet. Weird shadows. Anyone who's tried mountain biking at night will tell you that it definitely adds a new dimension of excitement and adventure to trails that you've ridden hundreds of times before. That's a big part of the appeal. So is the opportunity to get an evening workout when the days are short in the fall and spring and the trails are dry.

But the big dilemma is how to get started, what kind of lights to invest in, how much to spend. Perhaps the best recommendation is to go night riding with a friend who already has invested in high-tech, high-powered lights. You'll see the difference between trying to wing it with a low-powered headlight in front and a camping headlamp on your helmet, and the power of a high-wattage halogen or metal halide lighting system. Hence, for night riding, brighter is better and more fun because *you can see* ... what a concept!

However, bright lights are just as expensive as an entry-level mountain bike. The Cat Eye Stadium 3, for example, cost $450. It packs three times the punch of a halogen light with 6,000 volts of power, and its burn lift is about three hours. The latest NiteRider high-end model, the Blowtorch H.I.D., retails for $409. It has a handlebar-mounted system, four hours of riding time, and it's a favorite of 24-hour racers. If you're just getting into night riding, you might want to try a more medium-price lighting system, such as the NiteRider Evolution, which provides a helmet-mount or handlebar-mount, for about $150. Check with your favorite bike shop for their recommendations or check out lighting systems on the Internet. There are many options to consider.

Handlebar mounts for lights seem to be favored over helmet mounts because they provide better illumination of the trail. Helmet mounts provide better lighting on a trail with lots of curves and twists so you can see around the corner.

A couple tips to remember:

■Be sure to recharge batteries after you're through riding.

■In the winter, dress in layers and bring extra clothes for the ride. Be sure to protect your feet, too. You'll need to peel layers while climbing steep hills and then put the layers back on, along with a wind-proof shell, for freezing descents. It's amazing how fast your sweat can turn to ice on the downhills in the middle of winter.

MOUNTAIN BIKING WITH KIDS

When the time comes to raise a family, there's no reason for your mountain bike to collect cobwebs in the garage. After the baby arrives, consider investing in child-toting gear so your new child can enjoy the outdoors with you.

The latest toys — a baby trailer for infants and toddlers, and a Trail-A-Bike attachment for 3-year-olds and up — are tailor-made to maximize your children's safety and pleasure, while you and your partner enjoy the outdoors and get some exercise. Then, when your kids can pedal their own bike (and they start asking for a really cool and *really expensive* mountain bike) they'll hit the dirt or the pavement with their legs a-spinnin' and their faces a-grinnin'.

The ultimate set up: Dave and Jeanie Thomas pedal up Mountain Cove Road on their tandem with their son, Cassidy, riding in the baby trailer.

Parents will have to make the call as to when it's time to start taking their child cycling. The main concern, initially, is whether a child's neck is stable and strong enough to support the weight of a helmet, and endure the shaking action of a bumpy bike path or gravel road. Please consult your physician about these considerations. Typically, when children are six to eight months old, their neck may be stable enough for riding in a bike trailer. Just to be on the safe side, you can secure your child in a car seat for extra stability.

For extra visibility and safety, it's probably a good idea to buy an orange safety flag pole and attach that to the back corner of the baby buggy.

Here are some tips from veteran cycling parents for baby trailer trips:

■ Be sure your child is properly dressed for the weather — remember that they're just sitting there while you're generating body heat. Close the window flap to shield your child from the cold, rain and wind. Remember to apply liberal amounts of baby-specific sunscreen on their skin — they sunburn real easily. Have your child wear sunglasses when it's bright. If you're lucky, they'll keep the glasses on.

■ Feed your child before you go on a ride. Bring along extra food and drink.

■ Be prepared to tow some weight: 20 pounds for the buggy, plus your child's body weight, and a ton of miscellaneous stuff like diapers, extra clothes, toys, etc.

■ Be sure to bring along a variety of highly entertaining toys to keep your child happy and occupied. Noise-making toys work well. Kids may want to read or color, too. A baby buggy provides the advantage of giving a child his or her own space where these activities are possible.

■ Stay in communication with your child during the ride. Look back on a regular basis to see how they're doing. When they can talk, encourage them to tell you how they're doing. If you and your partner are riding together on separate bikes it may be a good idea for the person not towing the trailer to let you know if you're riding too fast or that your child needs attention.

Clay Lewis, 4, rides a Trail-A-Bike with his dad, Gregg.

■ Ride conservatively and give yourself plenty of time to stop. Remember that your turning radius is going to be much wider, and that you're towing extra weight.

■ Always keep the screen cover on the trailer to protect your child from projectiles launched from the back tire.

■ Use hand signals when riding on streets and observe the same traffic laws that pertain to vehicles. Ride with the flow of traffic.

■ Take your child on streets and pathways that are smooth and feel safe. Remember that many people driving cars and trucks don't even think you have a right to be there on the shoulder of the road.

WHERE TO GO:

■ The Greenbelt is a favorite destination, of course. With a new bike lane along Eckert Road, it's possible to do a loop around the river — from Municipal Park, just east of Broadway, to Eckert, across the river, into Barber Park, and then back to Municipal Park.

■ City streets that have good bike lanes, such as Hill Road, Warm Springs, Kootenai, 15th Street, and many others.

■ Some folks like to ride on the roads west of Meridian into the farm country. There aren't bike lanes per se, but there isn't nearly as much traffic. Dave and

Jeanie Thomas, the couple pictured on their tandem bike, like to ride the Greenbelt west of Ann Morrison Park, take the old railroad bridge across the river and the Greenbelt spur to Garden Street, and then they ride on Emerald to Meridian and beyond.

■ Dirt road rides in Military Reserve Park, Table Rock, Rocky Canyon Road and 8th Street. Hill climbs are much tougher when you're towing a trailer.

■ The Cartwright-Pierce Park-Hill Road Loop or the Cartwright-Dry Creek-Seaman's Gulch-Hill Road Loop. See the winter rides section in the back of the book for other possibilities.

TRAIL-A-BIKE OPTIONS

Trail-A-Bike attachments are a nifty new thing that allow your child to get accustomed to pedaling his or her own bike and getting a sense for balance and maneuvering. When you're climbing hills, your child can pedal, too. For adults, the Trail-A-Bike is a great invention that allows you to get a sweat-popping workout while bonding with your child.

Avid mountain bikers in this area don't hesitate to take their kids on the easier and smoother dirt roads and trails in the foothills. It's up to you to decide where to go, and what you're comfortable with. It's probably a good idea to pre-ride and scout places where you might want to take your child on a Trail-A-Bike.

Gregg Lewis, a longtime mountain biker in Boise, takes his son, Clay, who just turned 4, on rides in Military Reserve, Crestline, Corrals, the Greenbelt and Cartwright Road. "Clay loves the rolling dips and the whoop-de-doos," Lewis says. "There are days when he wants to go home and I want to keep going, and there are days when I'm ready to quit and he wants to keep going. I try to meet his needs."

Lewis outfits Clay with a helmet, sunglasses, cycling gloves, cycling shorts and sturdy hiking boots. The boots protect his son's feet and ankles from getting nailed by rocks and other obstacles. Lewis teaches him how to keep his feet in a parallel position -- at 9 o'clock and 3 o'clock -- to avoid hitting rocks.

Lewis brings along goo energy packs and power bars for Clay.

Other tips:

■ Communicate with your child frequently to ensure that he or she is having a good time. It should be a fun, positive experience, not a nightmare that will make them hate cycling forever.

■ Be sure to adjust the seat and handlebars to fit your child.

■ Use a good dose of common sense to know when to walk the bike when climbing and descending, and know when to return home.

■ Start on short rides and work up to longer ones.

■ It helps to have your partner ride with you to let the towing rider know when he or she is going too fast or the child is bouncing around too much.

GET ACTIVE WITH SWIMBA

VOLUNTEER EFFORTS CARVE OUT NEW TRAILS FOR YOU

In 1992, a group of local mountain bikers got the bright idea of forming a mountain bike advocacy group to promote responsible trail ethics, maintain trails and provide input on new developments to promote new additions to the Ridge to Rivers Trail Network. Today, the Southwest Idaho Mountain Biking Association (SWIMBA) has elected officers, a board of directors, money in the bank, and its mission has expanded to include many issues that advance the cause of mountain biking in Southwest Idaho.

Perhaps the most visible evidence of SWIMBA's work was the creation of a host of new trails in the Boise foothills in the 1990s. Prior to 1997 -- the first year that a part-time paid trail crew was hired to work in the foothills -- SWIMBA volunteers maintained a host of trails on a regular basis. In the fall of 1995, SWIMBA organized a group of volunteers to build Sidewinder Trail. The success of that project led to a more ambitious project in the spring of 1996 to build Shane's Trail, with the assistance of the Boise REI store, and several restaurants that provided food for volunteers. REI and SWIMBA teamed up again in May 1997 to rebuild Trail #1 in a new location after the old link to Bob's Trail and the Corrals Trail were bulldozed by fire-rehab tractors. SWIMBA volunteers, smokejumpers and other volunteers built a new loop (Redtail Ridge Trail) in the lower Dry Creek area in the summer of 1997. A key aspect of the Trail #1 and Dry Creek projects was that SWIMBA got grant funding to buy use of a Kabota tractor, which is a handy machine that rough-cuts a singletrack trail. Then volunteers come in afterward to shape the trail and install erosion control structures. In the late 1990s, SWIMBA teamed up with REI to build Kestrel Trail and Owl's Roost, opening more loops between Crestline and Hulls Gulch.

SWIMBA is involved in many other activities. Several SWIMBA members had a major role in the 2001 Foothills Open Space Campaign. In 2002, it co-sponsored the Tour de Fat event in Boise and raised more than $6,000 for future trail projects. SWIMBA also participates regularly in improving the Idaho City Park 'n Ski Areas.

SWIMBA usually meets on the third Wednesday of each month to discuss new projects and set priorities for action. To join SWIMBA, visit our web site, www.swimba.org, or call the current president, Harley Parson, at 389-9043.

Thanks a bunch!

RIDGE TO RIVERS

A VISIONARY PUBLIC TRAIL INITIATIVE

By Tim Breuer, *Ridge to Rivers Trail Coordinator*

The Ridge to Rivers Pathway System is a comprehensive network of trails, pathways and bicycle lanes throughout Ada County. Born from the desire to provide continued access to public lands, a comprehensive plan was developed with significant public input that proposed linking neighborhoods and public lands. The President's Commission on American Outdoors echoed this need by establishing "corridors of private and public recreation lands to provide people with access to open spaces close to where they live, and to link together the rural and urban spaces in the American landscape." The Ridge to Rivers Pathway System is a long-term project that seeks to achieve that goal.

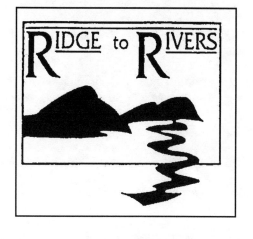

In April of 1992, seven local state and federal agencies formed a partnership to begin working toward implementation of the Boise Foothills Trail System.

The objective is to maintain and enhance recreation trails while protecting the fragile ecosystem in the Boise Front.

Today, there are more than 80 miles of trails accessible to the public that cross lands administered by the U.S. Forest Service, Bureau of Land Management, Idaho Department of Lands, Idaho Department of Fish and Game, the city of Boise, Ada County and private landowners. The trail network is so vast that a mountain biker can soar from the top of Bogus Basin over 4,000 vertical feet down any number of trails in the Front, and then follow pathways and bike lanes in the city of Boise to the Boise River Greenbelt. This is a unique opportunity that most communities could only dream about.

Due to the large amount of private land in the foothills, the success of the Ridge to Rivers program depends on the cooperation of private landowners, all government agencies and on the responsible conduct of trail users.

The program seeks to be a model of interagency cooperation and public/private partnerships that hopefully will become the norm in the years ahead.

For more information, see www.ridgetorivers.org.

IMAGE GALLERY

Jacob Collett of Cortez, Colo., soars off a bump in the Boise Foothills.

OK, what are the odds of crashing after big air and ending up with a custom-made Specialized tattoo on your forearm? Collett saw the parallel instantly.

Glenn Oakley

It's important to keep your focus on the here and now on Bob's Trail.

Kurt Holzer zooms down the Mores Mountain singletrack, near Bogus Basin.

Scott Van Kleek, left, and Bob Wood, are the studly mountain bike pioneers after whom Scott's Trail and Bob's Trail were named many moons ago. Both of them are still active riders, and they live in Boise.

Even springer spaniels like to walk the Oregon Trail loop. This is Maple Leaf on the Surprise Valley gravel trail, circa 1998.

The Red Fox trail is just minutes from downtown Boise, making it one of the most popular trails for dog-walkers, joggers and riders.

SWIMBA work crew builds the beginnings of the Redtail Ridge Trail in Hidden Springs in the summer of 1997. Pictured in the foreground are (left to right) Tom Baskin, Ron Stacy and Steve Stuebner.

Here's one of many creek crossings in Dry Creek. Wa-hoo!

Mark Lisk winds through the Black Forest in Military Reserve.

About Cyclocomputers

Trail mileage for this book was logged with a cyclocomputer. For maximum guidance, I recommend that cyclists follow the routes with a cyclocomputer. However, you don't need a computer to follow the beginner rides in the book or some of the intermediate out-and-back rides. Still, it's nice to have a computer to keep track of how far you've gone, actual riding time, and to keep tabs on your climbing speed and maximum speed on descents, of course.

Please recognize that cyclocomputers must be calibrated to the size of your wheel and tire pressure. Even after doing that, your computer readings may not match up with mine to the exact tenth of a mile. My own readings don't always match up to the exact tenth. Use common sense, and look for junctions within a few tenths of the actual mileage, and you should be OK.

About the Rating System

Quality: How the ride compares to other rides in an overall sense. Four stars denotes the highest quality. Included in this determination are the quality of mountain setting, how much shade or vegetation is present, the variety of riding conditions, the amount of singletrack trail involved (lots of singletrack gets a high rating), the type of climbing involved (if you have to hike, the ride loses a few points), the quality of panoramic views, and the amount of vehicle encounters along the way. Obviously, quality is a subjective term.

Distance: Total distance from start to finish or other points indicated. Some rides indicate one-way mileage if it's an up-and-back route.

Difficulty: Rides are organized according to location and ability. There are three basic categories: beginner, intermediate and advanced/expert. A beginner is defined as someone who recently purchased a mountain bike, and has little to no off-pavement riding experience. A beginner is expected to have very little endurance, especially related to climbing steeps. Intermediate riders are defined as those who ride off-pavement frequently, but are still working on building skills and endurance. Advanced and expert riders should have several years of experience on a mountain bike, well-honed climbing and downhill skills, and the capacity to ride at strenuous levels for several hours at a time. Because of the relatively steep terrain in the Boise foothills, even intermediate rides may seem surprisingly difficult.

Riding time: The amount of time required to complete a ride for the ability prescribed. The times are listed as a broad range to indicate that weaker riders will take longer than experts.

Trail: The riding surface: Two-track primitive jeep trails, four-wheel-drive roads, wide gravel roads, singletrack trails or hike-a-bike. All riding surfaces are dirt unless otherwise indicated.

Season: The time of year when the trail can be completed, in general terms.

Cautions: Special issues of concern.

Map Legend

————————	Paved Road or 2WD Dirt Road
··············	Jeep Trail or 4WD Dirt Road
– – – – – –	Single Track
(30)	US Highway
(72)	State Highway
555	Forest Service Road
🚶🚶	Hiking Trail
	Direction of Travel Indicator
6,000'	Elevation Marker
S F S/F	Trail Start/Finish Indicators
P	Parking
⛺	Campground
△	Mountain
⚲	Spring

THE RIDES

Graham Hill soars off a bump on Hard Guy Trail.

BOISE RIVER GREENBELT

Quality: ***
Distance: 17.1 miles
Difficulty: Easy -- all abilities
Riding time: 1-2 hours one-way
Trail: Paved path
Season: Year-round, weather permitting
Cautions: Yield to other users: walkers, joggers, roller-bladers, skiers.

The Boise River Greenbelt is one of the finest urban trails in the Northwest. Thanks to tireless efforts of visionary, dedicated Boise residents, businesses, developers and city officials, an extensive public pathway system has been reserved along the Boise River through all of Boise, most of Garden City and portions of Ada County. At the time of this publication, there were still significant gaps between Eagle Island State Park and west Boise. Future plans call for extending the pathway to Eagle Island Park, the original vision for the urban pathway. I urge Greenbelt users, particularly those who live in Eagle, to push their elected officials to make that vision a reality in the years to come.

The maps provided on the next two pages provide exploded views of the Greenbelt -- from points west of Glenwood to Broadway, and from Broadway to Lucky Peak. Parking symbols indicate the best places for public parking along the path. You'll notice that there are tons of options. Be creative about using the Greenbelt and look for loop opportunities near your home. The Hill Road-Greenbelt Loop is one obvious loop on the west portion of the path, and there is an excellent loop on the east end by starting at Boise State or Municipal Park, traveling out to Eckert Road on the north side of the river, and looping back toward town on the south side, via Barber Park, Wood Duck Island, the ParkCenter bike path, and bike lanes in River Run. People who live in the Columbia Village area have another loop possibility through their neighborhood, down the Idaho 21 connector to Surprise Valley, and then back to Columbia Village via Amity Road. All of these loops work well as winter rides.

When you use the Greenbelt, please observe the following code of etiquette prescribed by the government agencies that manage the pathway:

■ Pedestrians have the right of way at all times.

■ All Greenbelt users should stay to the right unless you're passing.

■ Pedestrians should not walk more than two abreast.

■ Motorized vehicles and hoofed animals are prohibited.

■ Dogs should be leashed.

■ Cyclists and in-line skaters should not use the Greenbelt at high speeds. Ride on the highway if you're interested in traveling at warp speed.

■ Cyclists should slow down when approaching pedestrians and notify them that you're about to pass by saying, "coming up" or "on your left."

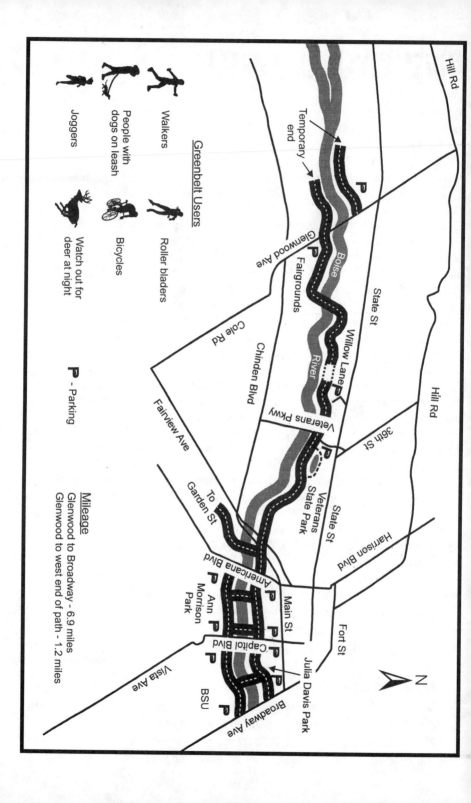

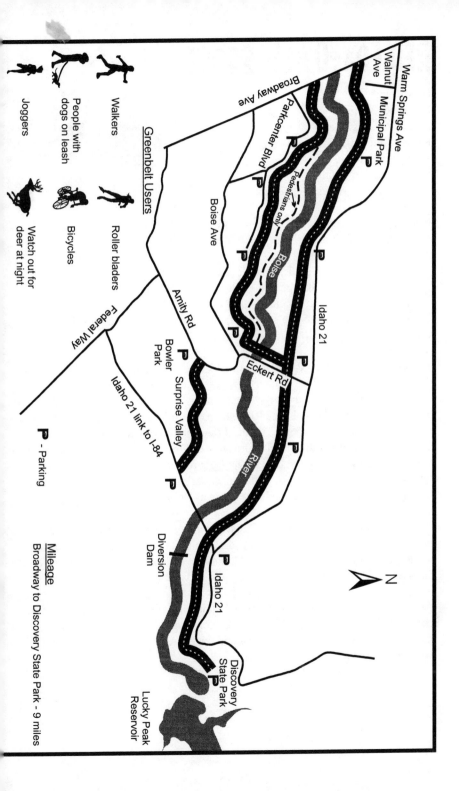

RED FOX-OWL'S ROOST

Quality: ***
Distance: 2.3 miles
Difficulty: Beginner
Riding time: 30 minutes and up
Trail: Singletrack
Season: Spring to fall
Watch out for: Hikers, joggers, dogs.

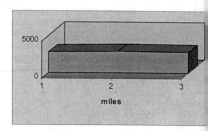

Getting there: From downtown Boise, head north on 9th Street to a dead end, adjacent to Camel's Back Park. The ride starts here.

The Ride: This loop provides an excellent introduction to mountain biking for beginning riders. You'll experience riding on loose sand, gravel, a few ruts and a short hill. This is also an excellent place to take kids for a bike ride. Watch for wildlife: The loop traverses a series of ponds teeming with songbirds in lower Hulls Gulch and a wooded grove on the way back.

To begin, head north on Red Fox Trail #36, ride to the left of the ponds, and then gear down to climb a short hill. Once on top, ignore the trails peeling off to the left and ride Red Fox toward the large water tank to the north. At mile .5, you'll come to a junction with the Chickadee Ridge loop. Consider that as an option the next time you ride the loop. At mile .8, you'll pass the water tank on your left, and then at mile 1, Chickadee Ridge loop returns to Red Fox. Ride to the left or right side of the gate ahead, cross 8th Street and bear right on the trail leading into the parking lot. Pick up Kestrel Trail #39A in the northeast end of the parking lot, next to a locked gate, and climb on a moderate grade as Kestrel snakes into the gulch.

At mile 1.3, turn right onto Owl's Roost and enjoy a slightly downhill cruise through Hulls Grove. At mile 1.5, a pedestrian trail (no bikes, please) branches off to the right, bear left on Owl's Roost. Ignore several neighborhood spur trails that come in from the left. Stay on the main trail and ride downhill.

At mile 1.9, Owl's Roost dumps out on 8th Street. Cross 8th Street directly and continue riding downhill along the creek. Now you're on Gold Finch Trail. Circle the ponds, or stop and watch the birds and ducks. After you return to the trailhead, you've covered 2.3 miles from the start.

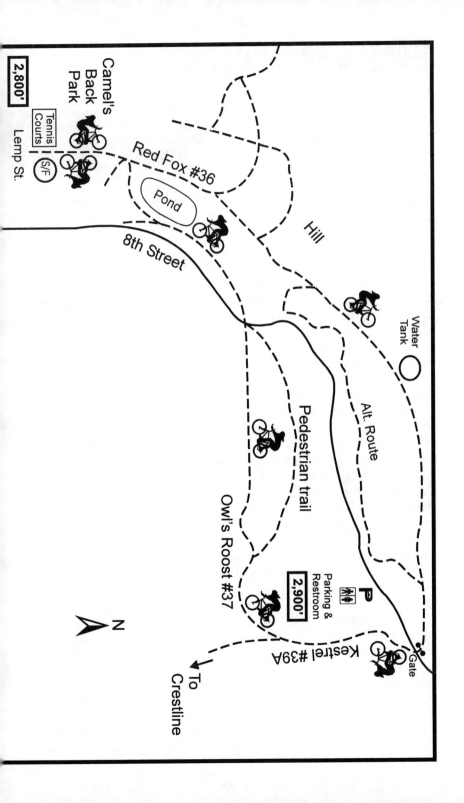

MORES MOUNTAIN LOOPS

Quality: ****
Distance: 4.3 to 11.2 miles
Difficulty: Beginner/Intermediate
Riding time: 1.5-2 hours
Trail: Single-track, 2WD dirt road
Season: May-October

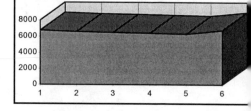

Getting there: From Boise, drive
to the junction of Harrison Boulevard and Hill Road, and go north on Bogus Basin
Road. Proceed about 16 miles to the lower lodge parking lot. The intermediate ride
starts here. Beginners should continue past the lower lodge on the Boise Ridge
Road for 3.3 miles to a junction for the Shafer Butte Picnic Area. Turn right and
drive to the picnic area parking lot. The beginner ride starts here.

The Beginner Loop: Head northeast out of the picnic area parking lot and search
for the Mores Mountain Trail, not to be confused with the Mores Mountain Interpretive Trail that runs for a quarter-mile (lined with wooden timbers) next to the
picnic area. The Mores Mountain Trail is a singletrack trail that heads for the east
slope of Mores Mountain, beyond the interpretive trail. Sorry, it's not well-marked,
but keep looking, you'll find it. Follow the singletrack trail on the east slope of
Mores Mountain for 1.5 miles, it's all slightly downhill. Enjoy the views of the
Grimes Creek country and Sawtooths way off in the distance. Keep your eyes on
the trail, however, because there will be a few technical and sandy spots. Go slow if
you feel uncomfortable. When the trail dumps onto the Ridge Road, turn left and
ride 1.6 miles to the junction with the picnic area access road. Turn left and climb
1.2 miles to the picnic area. You made it!

The Intermediate Loop: From the lower lodge, continue north on the Boise Ridge
Road past the cross-country lodge and a gate (may or may not be closed). At mile
3.3, you'll pass by the junction with the picnic area access road. Continue on the
ridge road to mile 5, where you'll see two wooden posts and a singletrack trail
peeling off to the right at a major corner. Watch carefully for the trail, it's not well-
marked. Turn right and follow the trail through brush and trees and enjoy the view.
It's a small-ring ride on a continuous uphill grade over a number of whoop-de-doos.
Exit the trail at 6.5 miles and cruise by the Mores Mountain interpretive trail. You
have arrived at the Shafer Butte Picnic Area. From here, turn right and descend 1.2
miles on the dirt road back to the Boise Ridge Road junction at 7.8 miles. Turn left
and ride 3.3 miles back to your vehicle at the lower lodge.

Interpretive remarks: In June and July, wildflowers create a plethora of colors on
the landscape. In the fall, cyclists will enjoy the bright variety of colors on shrubs
and trees — brilliant reds and yellows. Riders will notice granite spires rising from
the side of Mores Mountain, classic features of the Idaho Batholith granitic forma-
tion. Be sure to bring a lunch and enjoy the Mores Mountain area.

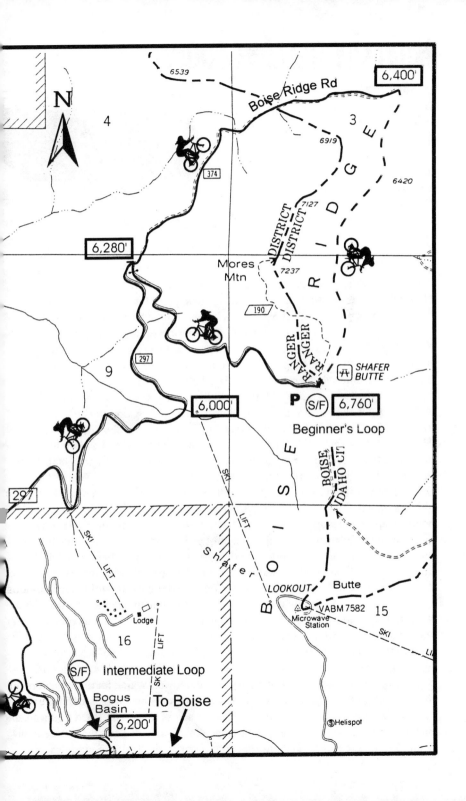

Military Reserve Loops

Quality: ****
Distance: 1.8 miles, short loop; 4.5 miles, long loop.
Difficulty: Beginner-Advanced
Riding time: 20 minutes to 1.5 hours
Trail: Singletrack, two-track
Season: Spring to fall
Watch out for: Walkers, joggers, horseback riders and dogs.

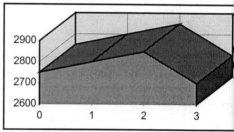

Beginner loop profile

Getting there: Ride or drive to Fort Boise Park at the junction of Reserve Street and Fort Street. Turn north on Reserve Street to Mountain Cove Road. Turn left. Park in the public lot on the left. The ride starts here.

General: Military Reserve, a city park, is a good place for beginners to get a feel for their mountain bikes on flat roads, and more hilly two-track and single-track trails. The park can be rich with wildlife. Listen for birds and watch for wildlife.

Easy loop: Ride up Mountain Cove Road, past the first right-hand bend, to the Toll Road trailhead #27A, and a gate on the right (mile .4). Ride around the gate, cross the creek and climb the two-track road for a half mile to a junction at mile 1.0. Turn right on Eagle Ridge Trail #25. It dips into the draw, crosses Cottonwood Creek and then bends right into a grassy meadow. Go straight on Cottonwood Creek Trail #27. At mile 1.5, bear left at an unmarked junction and enter the "Black Forest." The singletrack eventually skirts along the edge of the forest and a steep hill, above the creek. If you feel uneasy, please walk. It can be tough to balance on a narrow trail next to a steep dropoff. At mile 1.8, drop down into the Black Forest. New riders should walk this section. At the bottom, get back on your bike and enjoy a nice winding path through the woods. At mile 1.9, bear left as you emerge on the concrete apron, pick up a singletrack on the hillside to the left, and ride up on the gravel pathway adjacent to the flood-control cells. It's hard to believe in August, but Cottonwood Creek has flooded in the spring to the point where it could fill all the cells. Go right at mile 2.2, and ride back to the parking lot. End mileage: 2.5.

Advanced loop: Ride on Mountain Cove Road .4 miles to the Toll Road Trailhead #27A. Turn right and follow the two-track road to a junction at mile 1. Bear left on Trail #20, and climb a singletrack to the central ridge. The climb gets progressively steeper at mile 1.3. Once on top, enjoy a fun descent on Central Ridge Trail #22 back to the trailhead (mile 2.7). Turn left and go back to the Trail #20 - Trail #25 junction. Turn right, and follow #25 to the top of Eagle Ridge. It's a series of granny-gear climbs to the ridgetop and the radio tower. Watch for a trail peeling off to the left and descend back toward the flood-control ponds. Ride around the ponds, catch the singletrack into the Black Forest, cut across to the Toll Road trailhead, and pick up Trail #22 going up the middle ridge. Climb the ridge and then descend on Trail #20, the steep hill you climbed earlier, back to the Toll Road trailhead.

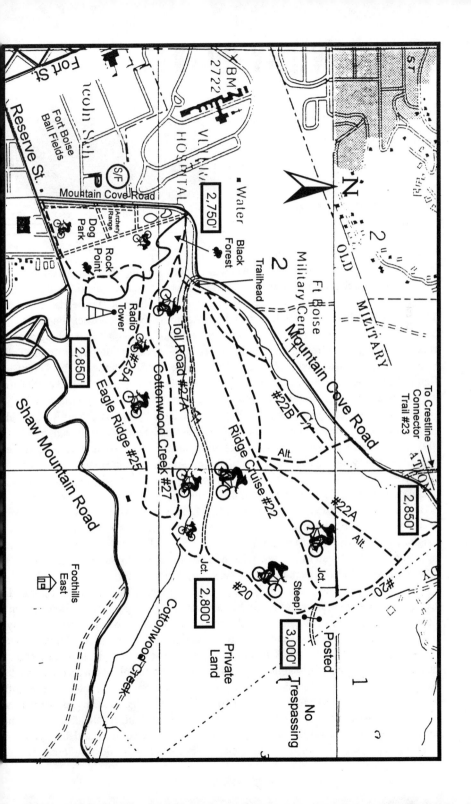

SURPRISE VALLEY-OR TRAIL

Quality: ***
Distance: 4.9 miles and up
Difficulty: Beginners and up
Riding time: 20 minutes to 1.5 hours
Trail: Two-track, singletrack
Season: April-October
Watch out for: Hikers, joggers and dogs. Please yield to all trail users.

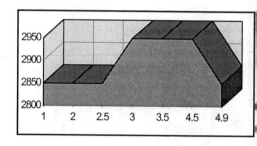

Getting there: Ride or drive to Barber Park. Mileage starts here. You can get there by taking the Greenbelt to Barber Park (on the north or south side of the river). Columbia Village residents will want to ride the loop in reverse, starting from the Whitman Trailhead.

The Ride: This is a nifty little historical loop that tours the Second Bench above Surprise Valley and Barber Pool and runs along the Old Oregon Trail on the upper rim. It was here that Oregon Trail emigrants took their wagons down the Kelton Ramp, a finely constructed rocky ramp. On this ride, you'll experience the Kelton Ramp. Most of the terrain on this ride is flat, suitable for beginners and all abilities.

To begin, at the junction of Boise Avenue and Eckert Road, turn right on Eckert, which turns into Amity Road around the corner. Take a left on Surprise Way at mile .4, and ride a mile to the Surprise Valley Community Center, where the singletrack gravel trail begins on the right, at the foot of the bluff (mile 1.4). Follow the gravel path as it cruises through sagebrush to the bottom of the Kelton Ramp (mile 2.0), walk your bike up the grade (city law), and soak up the interpretive signs at the top of the ramp (mile 2.2). Turn right, and follow the bike trail in a westerly direction. You'll reach the Whitman Trailhead at mile 3.1. This is an alternative entrance/exit point in Columbia Village. Continue to the west, and the two-tracks converge into a singletrack at a dead end on the bluff. Turn right and follow the singletrack down the steep hill to the water tank, and take the gravel road out to Surprise Way (mile 4.0). Turn left and head back to Barber Park. End mileage 4.9.

Long loop intermediate ride: From the east end of the Oregon Trail Reserve, take Lake Forest Drive to the Idaho 21-I-84 highway, cross the highway, and ride the paved road to the powerlines at the end of the parking lot. Mileage starts here. Hook up with a jeep trail to the left of the powerlines and head east. Turn right at mile .3, turn left at mile .4 and follow the jeep trail to the top of the third bench. Turn left at the top of the hill and cruise on the main two-track to a junction at mile 1.1. Bear left and descend into the gully, and then climb back to the Third Bench. At mile 1.7, hop over the gate and follow a four-wheeler track to the right. At mile 1.9 go left on the main two-track under the powerlines and follow it to a shot-up cattle trough at mile 3.2. This is the Bonneville Point junction. See page 68 for details from here.

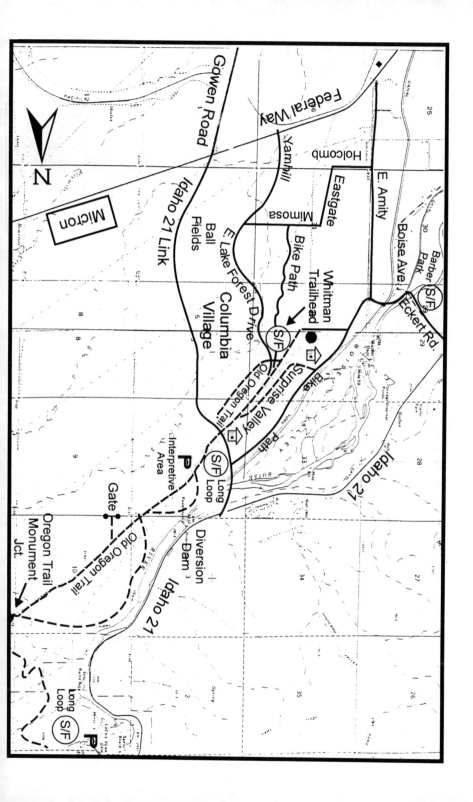

TOUR OF PEARL

Quality: **
Distance: 11 miles
Difficulty: Strong beginner to intermediate
Riding time: 1-2 hours
Trail: Dirt 2WD Road
Season: May to October
Watch out for: Cars, ghosts (just kidding), cattle, hunters.

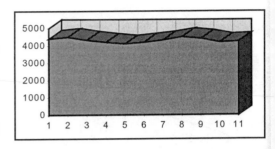

Getting there: Ride or drive to the top of Horseshoe Bend hill on Idaho 55. Park on the west side turnout (left side of the road as you're heading north). The ride starts here.

The Ride: This is a nice rolling cruise to the old mining town and present-day ghost town of Pearl. If you drop a shuttle rig in Eagle, it's also a great downhill ride from Idaho 55 to Pearl and eventually, north Eagle Road and the town of Eagle. This descent is about 18 miles long. If you want to do the whole thing on your bicycle, it's about 33 miles from Eagle, to the Horseshoe Bend Summit, and then back to Eagle via Pearl. That would be a good challenge for advanced cross-bike riders. The up-and-back ride is about 5.4 miles to a group of shanty buildings, old cars and rusty equipment in Pearl. The ride starts at 4,250 feet, and remains mostly level for the first couple miles. Then the road climbs several hundred feet to a junction on the left. Continue on the main road as it descends to Pearl (elevation 4,150). Find a good lunch spot. Several loops would be possible from Pearl except that private land is posted on both sides of the road, with multiple landowners. Return to Idaho 55 as you came, or do the long descent.

History: It's hard to imagine it today, but Pearl was a bustling gold-mining town 100 years ago with more than 100 residents. The first strikes in Pearl involved quartz. According to the late Idaho historian Merle Wells in his book, *Gold Camps and Silver Cities,* two quartz veins were worked in Pearl in the late 1860s, coinciding with the beginning of the gold-mining boom in the nearby Boise Basin. But apparently the interest in quartz dimmed, and Pearl did not receive strong interest until the 1890s. Wells wrote that between $30,000 to $80,000 worth of gold was recovered and sold between 1894 and 1896 in Pearl. Much of the mining occurred underground, as one can see from the evidence of mine shafts today. A deep shaft in Pearl was sunk over 1,000 feet in search of gold veins, but to no avail. Wells said a total of about 20,000 ounces of gold, worth $400,000 at the time, were removed from the Pearl region during the gold rush. The area is not active at the present time, although Wells hints that the Pearl mines were "not exactly worked out." Maybe someone with gold fever will revive the mines someday.

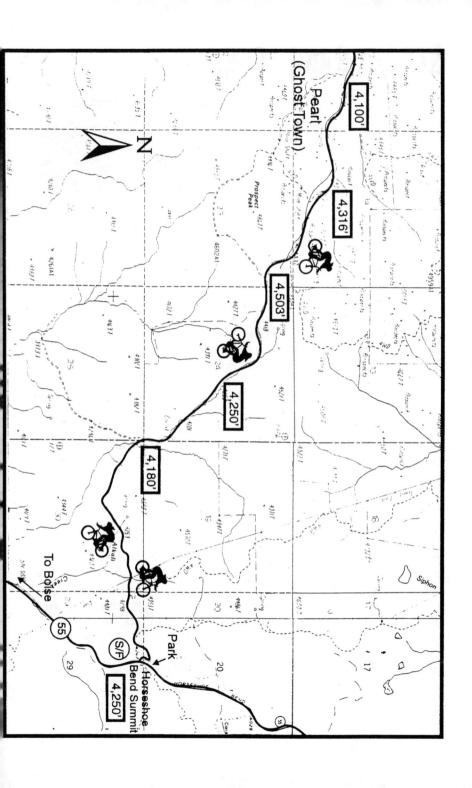

REDTAIL RIDGE LOOP

Quality: ***
Distance: Hidden Springs
beginner loop, 2 miles;
Redtail Ridge loop, 5.9 miles
Difficulty: Beginner, advanced intermediate
Riding time: 30 minutes-1.5
hours
Trail: 2WD dirt road,
singletrack
Season: April-October
Watch out for: Hikers and joggers
Topo map: Cartwright Canyon

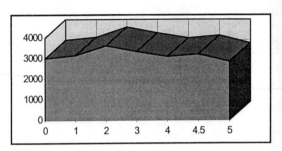

Getting there: Mileage for the Redtail Ridge Loop ride starts at the junction of Cartwright and Dry Creek roads. This junction can be reached via Cartwright Road from Bogus Basin Road (it's 5 miles to lower Dry Creek from Bogus Basin Road). Or, Hidden Springs can be reached via Seaman's Gulch Road (the road to the Ada County landfill). Take Seaman's over the top and then follow Lower Dry Creek Road, past Hidden Springs, to the junction with Cartwright Road.

The Ride: The loop described here is the first of many trails that will be developed in the Hidden Springs area as time goes on. The singletrack trails in the Redtail Ridge Loop Trail were created by SWIMBA and Hidden Springs volunteers, firefighters, and the Ridge to Rivers trail crew in 1997.

Redtail Ridge Loop: This trail can be accessed from Hidden Springs, Dry Creek Road or Cartwright Road. The mileage for the ride begins at the junction of Dry Creek and Cartwright roads. Ride up Cartwright Road 1.2 miles to a steep 4WD road on the left. Bear left on the 4WD road and climb a half mile to Redtail Ridge, named for a pair of red-tailed hawks that nest nearby. Continue on the two-track road until a singletrack trail bends off to the left at mile 2.2. It's a long downhill from here on the winding trail. You'll cross Current Creek at mile 3.3, and then climb a moderate grade to a set of hills overlooking Dry Creek Valley. Bear right at several junctions to stay with the longer ridge trail. At mile 4.3, the trail drops down to Dry Creek road, or you can stay high and do a little loop around a knoll before dropping down to Dry Creek Road (mile 5.0). Turn left and head back to the junction of Cartwright and Dry Creek at mile 5.9.

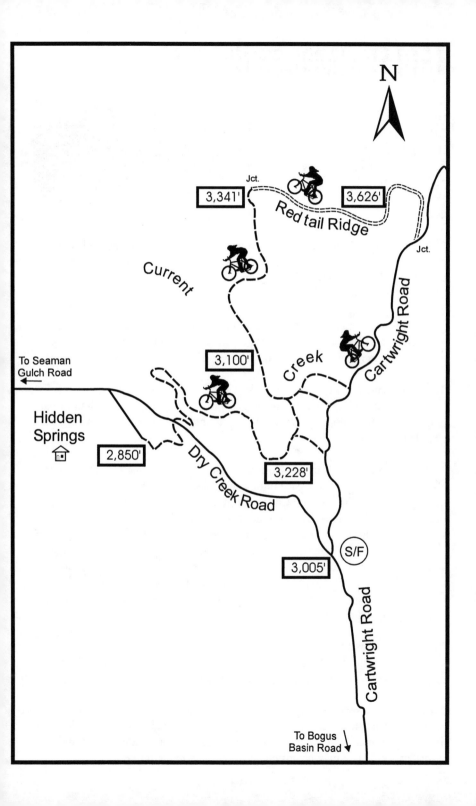

36th St.-Harrison Hollow

Quality: **
Distance: 2.5-plus miles
Difficulty: Intermediate and up
Riding time: 45 minutes-1.5 hours
Trail: Two-track, singletrack
Season: Spring to fall
Watch out for: Walkers, joggers, dogs.

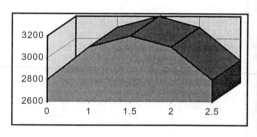

Getting there: To enter from Bogus Basin Road, ride to Harrison Hollow Road, just in front of Healthwise and next to the Harrison Hollow brew-pub parking lot on the left. Look for a dirt road heading up Harrison Hollow after the pavement ends. The ride starts here.

To enter from the 32nd Street side, watch for a gap in concrete jersey barriers on the north side of Hill Road directly across from 32nd Street (This access works only for people who are riding to the trail; there's no parking here) The ride starts here.

The Ride: This fine little trail network exists due to the tolerance of several landowners, including the Simplot Co., Healthwise, and Richard B. Smith Real Estate. These trails don't go far, but if you double or triple the loops, you'll get an excellent workout.

To begin, proceed up Harrison Hollow 1 mile to a saddle junction. The jeep trail climbs at a very reasonable pace until a short steep spot before the saddle. From here, go right to climb toward Cartwright Road and link up with the ridge cruise back to Harrison Hollow. This is a nice short loop. Watch out for private homes as you make the short loop. For a longer ride, go left at the top of the saddle and then bear right on the singletrack. Now, you're going to cruise along several ridgeline singletrack trails toward 32nd Street, Hillside School and Quail Hollow Golf Course. If you start at 32nd Street or Hillside School, follow the trail up the ridgeline to the top of the hill and ride the ridge spine toward the east to Harrison Hollow or the ridge cruise.

Please! If you take the Harrison Hollow ridge trail back toward Healthwise, please walk your bike around the new homes under construction. And please do not ride on the grass or landscaping areas around the Healthwise building.

Note: There are several trails on Richard B. Smith Realty property on the southern-most side of this trail network that end by 28th Street and Hill Road. These areas are not recommended for public use because the trails are badly eroded and unsustainable. They may be posted no trespassing in the future.

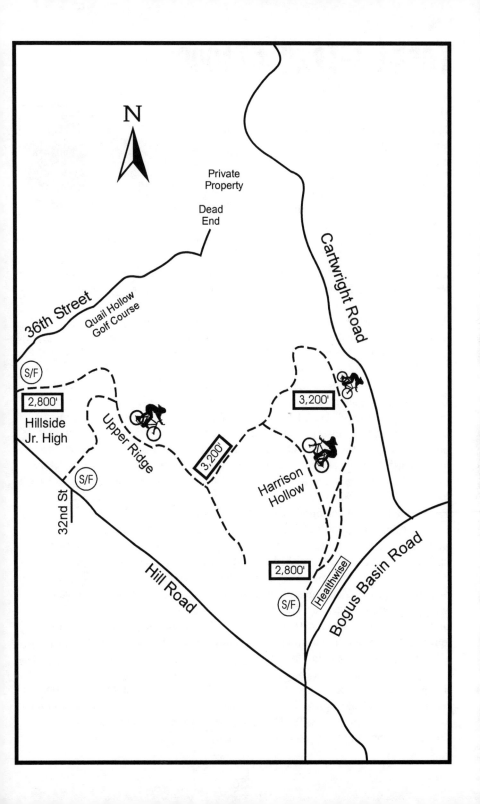

CORRALS-TRAIL #1 LOOP

Quality: ***
Distance: 7.3 miles
Difficulty: Advanced intermediate
Riding time: 1.5-2.5 hours
Trail: Two-track, singletrack
Season: April-October
Trail also open to: Runners, walkers and horseback riders; please yield to all trail users. Uphill riders have the right of way!

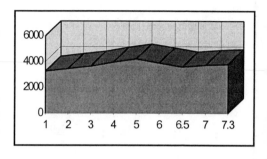

Getting there: Ride or drive to Highlands School at the intersection of Bogus Basin Road and Curling Drive. Park in the school parking lot. The ride starts here.

The Ride: Proceed up Bogus Basin Road about 1.8 miles to a gate and a dirt road on the right. This is the beginning of the Corrals Trail. You are now entering private property. The J.R. Simplot family has been very generous to allow public use of this trail. Please respect private property, don't litter and tread lightly. Follow the dirt two-track road as it climbs across the lower foothills and then drops into Crane Creek. Note the gate at the wooden corrals at 3.2 miles. This is the junction with "Hard Guy/Fast Guy" Trail. Proceed to the right on the Corrals Trail and enjoy a brisk downhill to a metal gate at 3.7 miles. Open the pedestrian gate and close it behind you. Now the trail climbs at a fairly steep rate to a saddle. Conserve energy and downshift to an easy gear. At mile 4.6, there's a steep switchback just before the saddle. At 4.9 miles, you'll reach the saddle. Take a minute to catch your breath. Look to your left: that's Scott's Trail, a singletrack trail that climbs to 8th Street. Proceed to the right and climb one more short hill to the summit of the Corrals route. At this point, you've climbed 1,600 vertical feet over 5 miles. Now, it's pretty much all downhill to the junction with Bob's Trail, and then you'll have to spin up a short climb on Trail #1 back to 8th Street. From the summit, proceed with caution on the eroded singletrack down a series of steep hills -- the trail is rutted and washboard-prone. You'll go around a BLM gate at mile 6.2. Keep riding on the wide singletrack (you're on Trail #1 now) and watch for a hairpin turn to the right and a well-vegetated gully. This is the Bob's Trail (Trail #30) junction, for future reference. It's a continuous modest climb now for a little less than a mile on Trail #1 to the junction with 8th Street.

From 8th Street, you've got several options. You can cross the road and drop into Hulls Gulch and take either Hulls, Crestline, Kestrel or Red Cliffs back 8th Street, or you can take Crestline to the Military Reserve Connector Trail and descend into Boise from that direction. You make the call.

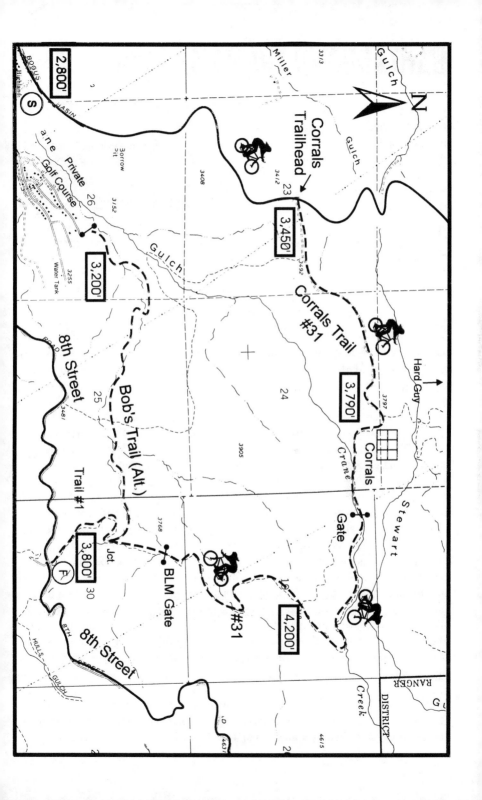

BANZAI DOWN THE BOISE FRONT

Quality: ****
Distance: 16.4-17.7 miles
Difficulty: Intermediate and up
Riding time: 1-3 hours
Rating: Jeep trail, singletrack
Season: May-October
Topo maps: Boise North, Shafer
Butte, Robie Creek

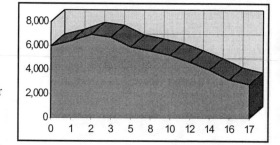

Getting there: From the corner
of Bogus Basin Road and
Curling Drive, ride your bike or drive about 13 miles up Bogus Basin Road to a
pullout and parking area on the right side of the road. Mileage for the ride starts
here.

The Ride: The "Banzai" concept was first developed by Idaho Mountain Touring
as a cool, end-of-the-season race, starting from the top of the Deer Point Chairlift
and finishing in Hyde Park. I'm including it here with several downhill options off
the Boise Ridge Road because it's such a kick to experience a massive descent of
4,000 vertical feet (6,800 feet to 2,750 in Boise). Many riders simply don't have the
endurance to climb to the Boise Ridge, but most can handle a two-mile climb --
even if you have to walk some of it -- knowing there's a one-of-a-kind experience
ahead. This ride gives everyone who tries it a sense of the magic, to realize we have
a mountain trail system of this breadth and magnitude right here in our backyard.
Try this ride and fly like an eagle -- extend your wings and swoop down with the
force of gravity to your home. **To begin,** pedal out of the pullout area and take an
immediate right on the service road to Deer Point and the Boise Ridge Road. It's a
continuous uphill climb of 2.1 miles to the ridge road junction. Turn right and begin
the flight down the Boise Ridge Road to either the Hard Guy Trail #33 (mile 7.8), a
challenging singletrack descent for advanced and expert riders, or pedal on to 8th
Street (mile 9.6), which is the original Banzai route and the preferred route for
intermediate riders. <u>Regardless of which route you choose, be sure to bear right at
the first two-way junction to stay on the ridge road.</u> **Don't miss that turn.** The 8th
Street route involves a 1.8-mile climb over "The Big Hill" from the junction with
Hard Guy to the top of Eagleson Summit. But the downhill involves no technical
aspects, even though it may shake your teeth loose. <u>Be sure to keep your speed in
check on both trails to avoid injury.</u>

A couple tips for 8th Street riders: Follow the sign for 8th Street at the Crooked
Summit junction. Bear right at a major three-way junction at mile 9.4. The turnoff
for 8th Street is marked by a junction of Trail B and D. Turn right on Trail B.

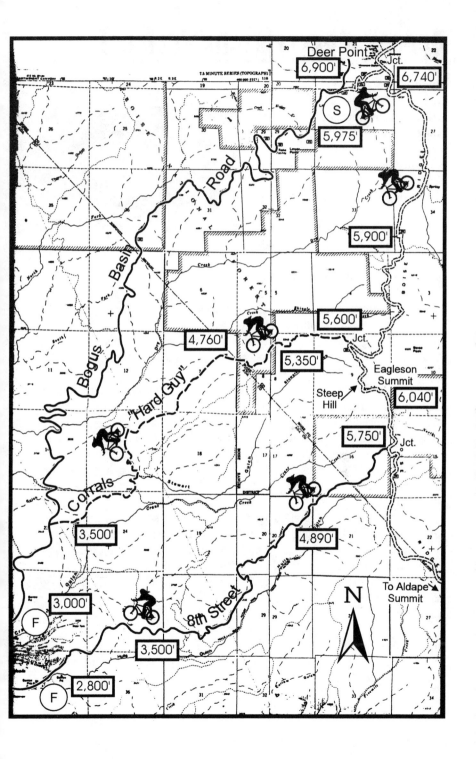

REDFOX-CRESTLINE-RED CLIFFS

Quality: ***
Distance: 5.5 miles
Difficulty: Intermediate
Riding time: 30 minutes-1 hour
Trail: Singletrack, two-track
Season: April-October
Watch out for: Joggers, hikers, horses, dogs and mountain bikers

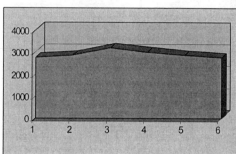

Getting there: Ride or drive to Camel's Back Park or the north end of 9th Street. The ride and mileage start at the beginning of Red Fox Trail #36.

The Ride: Here's a short intermediate ride for folks who are looking for a relatively easy loop that doesn't require much time away from home or work. Pick up Red Fox Trail #36 at the north end of 9th Street and the extreme east end of Camel's Back Park. Follow Red Fox as it proceeds north past the ponds in Lower Hulls Gulch, climbs a short hill and heads for a water tank and 8th Street. You'll pass the junction with Chickadee Ridge at .6 miles. At mile 1.1, ride around the gate, cross 8th Street, bear right into the parking lot, and pick up Kestrel Trail #39A, next to a locked gate, heading east up the gully. It's a mile of climbing on an easy to medium grade to Crestline Trail #28. At the top, (mile 2.2) turn left on Crestline, and ride to a left-hand turn for the Red Cliffs Trail #39 (mile 2.7). Now you're heading downhill on Red Cliffs back to Hulls Gulch. Watch out for man-and bike-eating ruts, steep descents, loose sand and other trail obstacles. At mile 3.0, bear left and climb to the top of the hill, and then enjoy a fast descent. At mile 4.0, the trail bends to the left and you'll ride through deep red sand. Try to stay on the well-traveled path in the middle. Shift your weight to the rear and keep your hands off the brakes in this section. At the bottom of the hill, turn left and head back to Camel's Back. When Trail #29 approaches the Hulls Gulch parking lot, bear right, cross 8th Street, ride around the gate and pick up Red Fox (mile 4.3). Follow Red Fox Trail #36 back to the 9th Street trailhead or Camel's Back Park. You made it! End mileage: 5.5 miles.

Interpretive remarks: The construction of Kestrel Trail and portions of Redcliffs occurred in the late 1990s as part of a SWIMBA project in cooperation with the Boise REI store, Tim Breuer and the Ridge to Rivers Trail Program, and other sponsors.

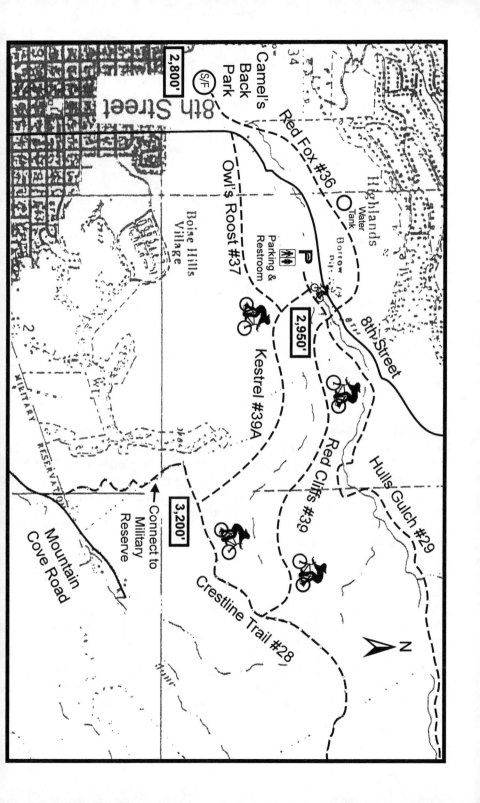

CRESTLINE-HULLS GULCH LOOP

Quality: ****
Distance: 4.5-6 miles
Difficulty: Intermediate and up
Riding time: 1-2 hours
Trail: Two-track dirt road; single-track dirt path
Season: April-November
Trail also open to: Runners, walkers, horseback riders, motorcycles; please yield to all trail users. Uphill bicyclists have the right of way!

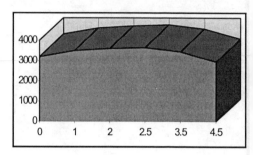

Crestline-Hulls Gulch Loop profile

Getting to Hulls Gulch: To start the loop in Hulls Gulch, ride to Boise's North End (north of downtown) and go north on 8th Street. After the road turns to dirt, continue about one mile to a trailhead on the right for Hulls Gulch Trail #29, adjacent to the parking lot.

Getting to the Crestline trailhead: To start the loop on Crestline Drive, ride to the North End and follow 8th Street to Brumback Street. Turn right, and follow the road to Crestline Drive. Turn right again and climb to a broad dirt turnout and a trailhead for the Crestline Trail (#28). The ride starts here.

The Ride: Intermediate cyclists should ride this loop starting at Crestline. The climb is much easier and flatter than riding up Hulls Gulch. More experienced riders will enjoy the challenge of riding up Hulls Gulch. **Beginning at the 8th Street junction** with the Hulls Gulch trail, cruise up the sandy single-track trail into the canyon. The trail rolls mostly up and down the gulch on the left side of the creek. Most riders will find a comfortable pace in low gear. Conserve energy: it's 800 vertical feet of climbing to the Crestline junction. As you're climbing, watch out for poison ivy hanging over the trail. Riders also will have to lift their bikes over at least one rock pile. Be aware that there may be mountain bikers storming down the trail who don't have a clue about trail etiquette. Make them yield so they learn that uphill cyclists have the right of way. **At the Crestline-Hulls junction,** you'll see a BLM sign. From here, riders can either loop back to Crestline or, if you want to enhance the workout, climb another half-mile and 200 vertical feet to the motorcycle parking lot on 8th Street. Turn around and descend to the Crestline-Hulls junction and ride down the Crestline Trail. It's about 2.5 miles to Crestline Drive. On your way down, you'll notice the junction with Trail #4 and Sidewinder Trail #24. Be sure to yield to walkers, joggers and other mountain bikes as you cruise down the trail. It's a hoot. To return to 8th Street, turn right off of Crestline on either the Red Cliffs Trail or Kestrel Trail. Enjoy!

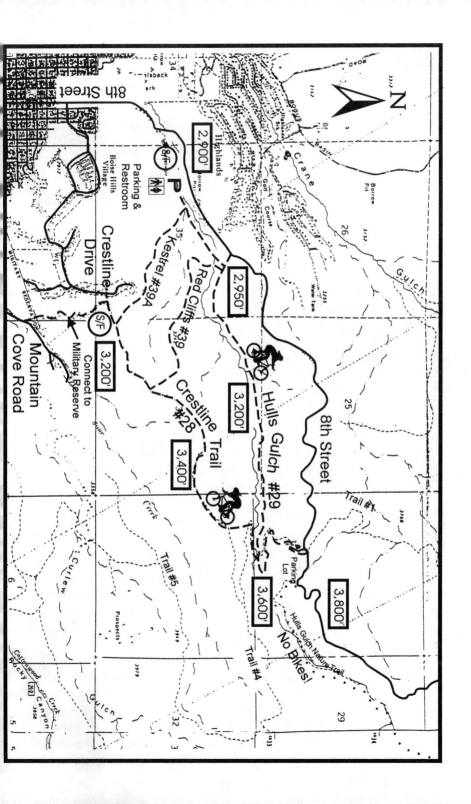

SHANE'S TRAIL LOOP

Quality: ***
Distance: 3.5 miles and up
Difficulty: Intermediate
Riding time: 30 minutes-1.5 hours
Trail: Singletrack
Season: April-October
Watch out for: Hikers and joggers

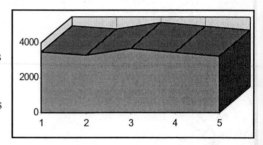

Getting there: This trail starts .6
miles after the end of the pavement on Rocky Canyon Road. There's no parking at the trailhead, so it's best to ride your bike to the trail, or park a vehicle at the end of the pavement on Rocky Canyon Road. To reach those destinations, go north on Reserve Street, parallel to Fort Boise, and turn right onto Shaw Mountain Road. It's two miles to the junction of Shaw Mountain and Table Rock roads. Veer left to access Rocky Canyon Road.

The Ride: Shane's Trail is a sweet, short loop trail that provides a tour of the lower reaches of the grassy foothills about a mile above Military Reserve Park. Shane's only gets three stars because it has no shade, and it can get piping hot on the south slope in the heat of July and August. The trail is named for Shane Erickson, a promising young lad who worked at Idaho Mountain Touring and regularly took part in SWIMBA trail projects. Tragically, Shane died in a car wreck in the winter of 1996. So when SWIMBA teamed up with REI to build a new trail in April 1996, it seemed appropriate to name it for Shane Erickson. **To begin,** follow Rocky Canyon Road to the end of the pavement. As you begin the climb up the canyon, watch for Shane's junction (Trail #26A) on the left at mile .6. Ride the steep approach to Shane's or carry your bike. Spin up the switchbacks to an initial saddle at mile .9. Watch for the loop junction in 100 yards and bear left to do the loop clockwise. The trail snakes across the foothills on a fairly level contour for a bit, and then it descends to the bottom of the loop at mile 2. Bear right and honor the no trespassing signs. The trail contours around a draw and then begins to climb. At mile 2.5, Trail #26 peels away to the left to connect to Trail #5 (see below). Shane's Trail winds to the right and climbs to a summit at mile 2.9. Now it's a fun descent back to the loop junction and then back to Rocky Canyon Road. The total loop mileage back at the end of the pavement is 4.6.

Shane's Trail is the only link to the lower end of Trail #5. So if you're riding Trail #4-Trail #5 from the Boise Ridge Road, be sure to follow Trail #26 back to Shane's Trail (#26A) and finish out on Rocky Canyon Road. It's slightly less than a mile from the #26-#26A junction to Trail #5. If you're interested in a longer climb than Shane's offers, consider taking Trail #26 to Trail #5 and then climbing Trail #5 to Trail #4 (3.6 miles of steep climbing). If you like to climb, it's worth it.

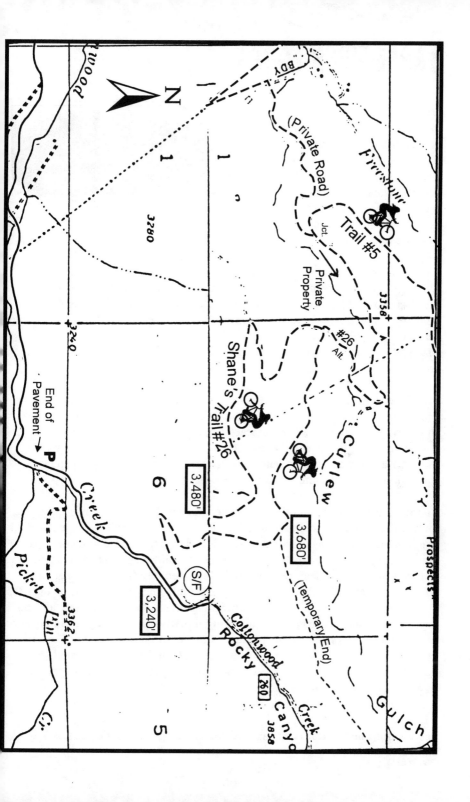

TABLE ROCK LOOPS

Quality: ***
Distance: 4.5-6 miles
Difficulty: Intermediate-Advanced
Riding time: 30 minutes-2 hours
Trail: Singletrack, two-track
Season: April-November
Trail also open to: Runners, walkers, horseback riders, motorcycles; please yield to all trail users. Uphill bicyclists have the right of way!

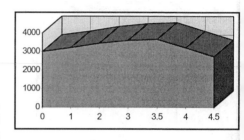

Table Rock Rd.-S. Face-State Pen profile

Getting there: The Table Rock trail complex has several good access points: Quarry View Park, just north of Warm Springs Avenue; the old state penitentiary area has good parking and a trailhead, or Table Rock Road itself, accessed by climbing Shaw Mountain Road in Foothills East. To reach Quarry View and the old state pen, watch for a left-hand turn off Warm Springs Avenue, just east of the M&W Market. Park at Quarry View or behind the Bishop's House in the old pen compound. The ride starts here.

The Ride: The Table Rock area offers a rich network of trails in a compact setting. There's something for riders of nearly all abilities to enjoy here. Intermediate riders should ride up Table Rock Road to reach the top on a broad paved road with a couple of steep hills. Even if the road gets too steep, you won't have to walk for long. Advanced riders should start from the Old Pen and attempt the south face "grunt" trail, which features a stout, in-your-face climb.

To tour Table Rock from the old state pen, ride up Trail #15, a single-track trail, toward Table Rock. Ignore trails on left unless you want to explore Castle Rock. At .4 miles, the trail levels out for a moment, then climbs toward the south face. At .9, ignore a single-track trail on the right. Stay on the trail and climb to a junction with Trail #16 at 1.1 miles. Turn right on Trail #16 and enjoy a flat cruise under the powerline. (Stay on Trail #15 to do the "grunt" trail). On Trail #16, stay on the left trail and follow the contour above Warm Springs Mesa. At 1.6 miles, stay left and angle toward an upper saddle. **You are now on private property. The landowner requests that riders stay on the trail and stay out of the subdivision.** The trail gets very steep at this point; conserve energy. At 2.1 miles, stay left again to head up to Table Rock. At 2.6 miles, you'll come to the main quarry road. Stay to the right and avoid the quarry. You'll reach the top of Table Rock at 3.3 miles. Return via the south face or Table Rock Road.

See Foothills on the Rocks on page 102 for another great loop ride on Castle Rock and Table Rock.

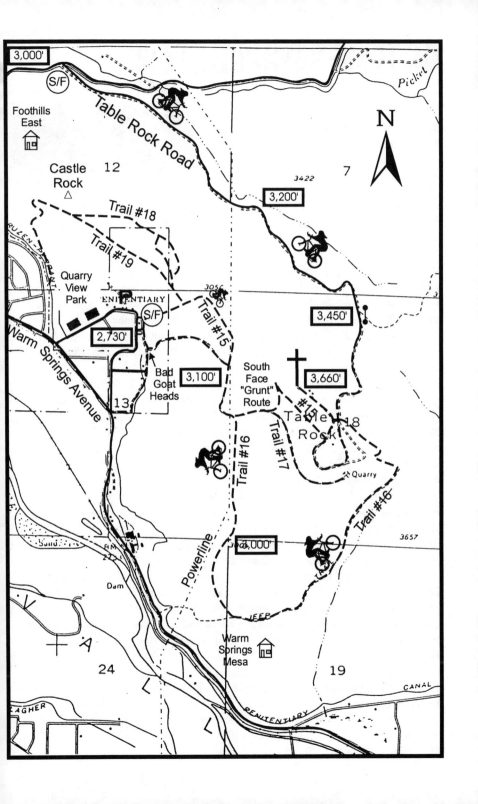

OR TRAIL-BONNEVILLE POINT

Quality: ***
Distance: 9.6 miles, out and back
Difficulty: Intermediate
Riding time: 1.5-2.5 hours
Trail: Two-track dirt road
Season: Spring to fall

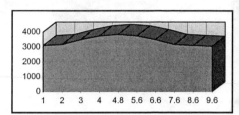

Getting there: Ride or drive to the top of Lucky Peak Dam. Turn right and park in the first parking lot on the left after you cross the dam. The ride starts and finishes here.

The Ride: This ride wraps around the mountain from Lucky Peak Dam and eventually connects to the Old Oregon Trail route, east of Boise. Eventually, the trail rises to Bonneville Point, the grassy knoll from which Oregon Trail emigrants viewed the Boise Valley for the first time after a long, extremely arduous and dusty trip across the Snake River Plain. Get ready for a fair bit of climbing -- an 850-foot vertical rise over 4.8 miles to the BLM Bonneville Point interpretive site.

To begin, cross the paved road by the parking lot entrance and ride downhill on a gravel road for about 200 yards to a junction. Turn left and head for the foothills. At .3 miles, turn right at a junction next to the bluff. Now you're on the main road to the Oregon Trail. It descends and then climbs gradually along the slope to a bench above the river. At .6 miles, cross the Corps of Engineers gate. (Despite the message on the gate, the public can use the trail from 6 a.m. to 11 p.m. Increased safety measures were installed around Lucky Peak in light of the 9/11 incident). Continue on the road to a three-way junction at 2 miles. Look for the Oregon Trail monument, a four-foot concrete peg. To ride back to Boise along the Oregon Trail, go right. To reach Bonneville Point, turn left and climb the two-track road for about a mile until you reach a flat spot. At 3.3 miles, a side trail comes in from the left. This is a steep route back to the gate. Continue on the flat ridge for .7 miles; watch for the last 100-foot hill ahead. Stay to the right for the most gradual grade to Bonneville Point picnic area at 4.8 miles. Signs and plaques at the picnic area provide historical details on the Oregon Trail, the key route for over 300,000 emigrants in the mid-1800s. This site is accessed by vehicle via Black's Creek Road, just east of Boise on I-84. It's possible to rendezvous with your family for lunch here.

From Bonneville Point, cyclists can take a short side trip of 1.4 miles round-trip to a bunch of electric towers. Return to Bonneville Point and cruise back toward Lucky Peak the way you came; it's 4.8 miles back down the jeep trail to Lucky Peak.

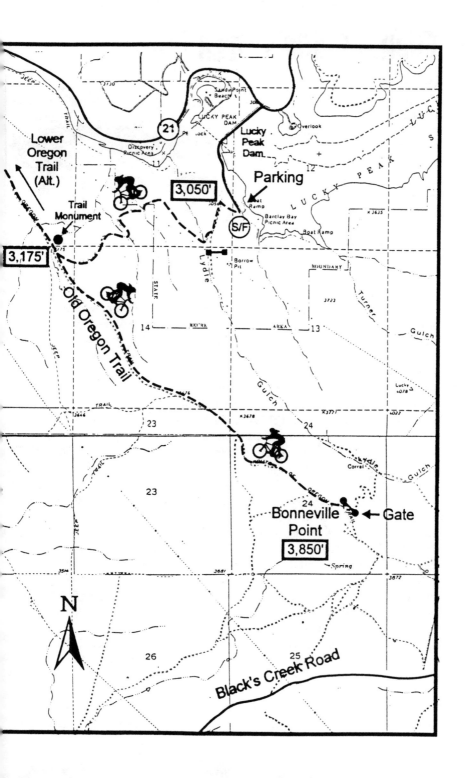

CORRALS-BOB'S TRAIL

Quality: ****
Distance: 8.4 miles
Difficulty: Advanced/expert
Riding time: 1.5-2 hours
Trail: Two-track, singletrack
Season: April-October
Trail also open to: Runners, walkers & horseback riders; please yield to all trail users.

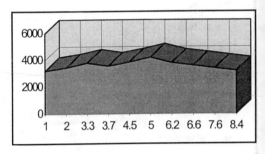

Getting there: Ride or drive to Highlands School at the intersection of Bogus Basin Road and Curling Drive. Park in the school parking lot. The ride starts here.

The Ride: Proceed up Bogus Basin Road about 1.8 miles to a gate and a dirt road on the right. This is the beginning of the Corrals Trail. You are now entering private property. The J.R. Simplot family has been very generous to allow public use of this trail. Please respect private property, don't litter and tread lightly. Follow the dirt road as it climbs across the lower foohills and then drops into Crane Creek. Note the gate at the wooden corrals at 3.2 miles. This is the junction with Hard Guy/Fast Guy Trail. Proceed on the Corrals Trail and enjoy a brisk downhill to a metal gate at 3.7 miles. Pass through the side gate. Now the trail climbs at a moderate to steep grade to a saddle. At mile 4.6, you'll climb a steep switchback just before the saddle. Once on top, proceed to the right and climb one more short hill to the Corrals summit. At this point, you've climbed 1,600 vertical feet over 5 miles. Now, it's pretty much all downhill to the junction with Bob's Trail. Beware of cracks and gullies in the trail on the downhill sections. You'll go around a BLM gate at mile 6.2. Keep riding on the singletrack (you're on Trail #1 now) and watch for a hairpin turn to the right and a well-vegetated gully. This is the Bob's Trail #30 junction. Turn right, and follow the narrow path as it snakes along next to the East Fork of Crane Creek. Be prepared for a technical trail with many obstacles that have a tendency to pitch riders off their bikes or over their handlebars. I once had a nasty spill into a big grove of poison ivy here. About two-thirds of the way down Bob's, the trail crosses the crest of a new 50-foot-high dam that was built for flood-control purposes in the fall of 1997. Then, the trail drops down a steep hill into the creek bottom, amid tall boulders and many other rocks, creating fun but challenging riding. Eventually, the trail ends and dumps out on a cul de sac. Turn left and follow the pavement to Braemere, turn right and ride downhill to Curling Drive and Highlands School.

Interpretive note: Bob's Trail is named for Bob Wood, a mountain bike pioneer who still lives in Boise. The trail was originally developed as a livestock trail.

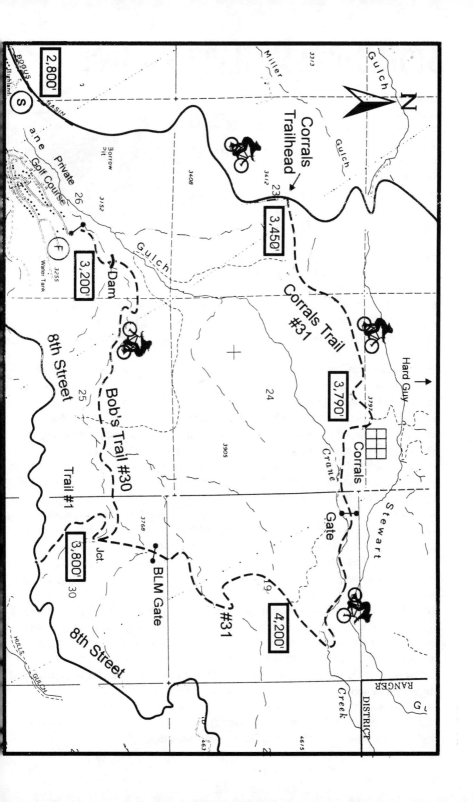

Scott's-8th St.-Hard Guy Loop

Quality: ****
Distance: 18.2 miles
Difficulty: Advanced
Riding time: 2-4 hours
Trail: Singletrack, two-track
Season: Spring to fall
Hazards: Watch out for out-of-control vehicles on 8th Street, deep ruts on Boise Ridge Road.

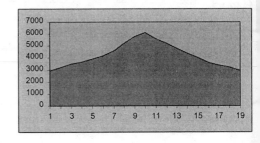

Getting there: Ride or drive to Highlands School at the intersection of Bogus Basin Road and Curling Drive. Park at the school. The ride starts here.

The Ride: It's a grunt to climb Corrals, Scotts, and 8th Street to Eagleson Summit, but there's a big reward on the totally fast and fun descent on Hard Guy Trail. It's all singletrack. This is one of the author's favorite loops in the foothills.

To begin, ride up Bogus Basin Road 1.8 miles to a dirt road and gate on the right. This is the trailhead for Corrals Trail #31. Cruise up the Corrals Trail to the saddle junction with Scott's Trail (mile 4.8). You will encounter two gates; be sure to close the gates behind you. At the saddle junction, turn left and ride Scott's to 8th Street (mile 5.9). Scott's is a fairly steep and narrow singletrack. Conserve energy. Turn left on 8th Street and climb the dirt road for another two miles to the junction with the Boise Ridge Road (mile 7.9). The grade is fairly steep the whole way. Enjoy the pine scent, shade, wildflowers and bird song as you climb into the forest ecozone. Turn left on the Ridge Road and enjoy a more up-and-down cruise as you pass by a number of broken-down cabins. At mile 8.1, you'll come to a Y-junction with a ridge road spur. Turn left and ride toward Eagleson Summit. In the last half-mile, the grade climbs again to the summit at mile 9.0. From this point on, it's pretty much downhill the whole way! Great views of the Treasure Valley and the Owyhee Mountains can be seen from here.

Blast downhill on the Ridge Road for a mile -- watch out for big ruts, sometimes it's best to jump them. At mile 9.9, you'll come to a sharp right-hand corner, and the junction with Hard Guy Trail #33 on the left. Take a breather, a munchie break and soak up the scenery. Get ready for one of the best downhills in the Boise Foothills. You'll zip down 3,000 vertical feet in no time. The singletrack snakes along the Hard Guy ridge all the way. It's 4.5 miles of sheer fun to a gate near a fork of Crane Creek (mile 14.4). Cross the creek at mile 14.6, and then climb a singletrack switchback to the Corrals Trail (mile 15). Turn right and head back to Highlands School (mile 18.2). You've earned your supper.

72

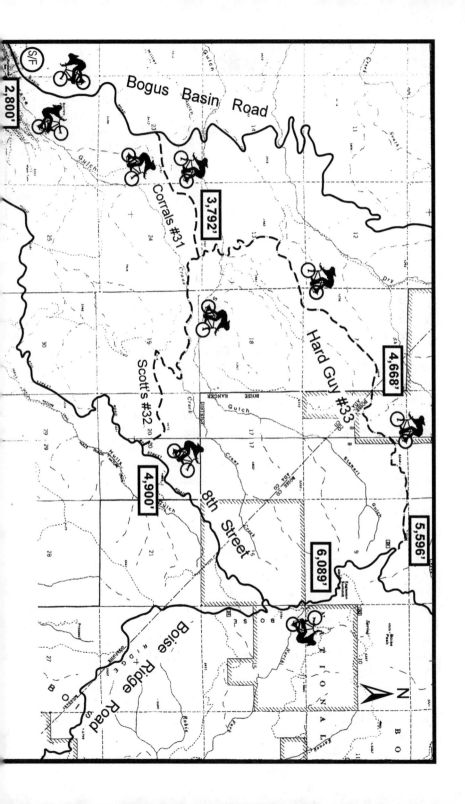

TOUR DE BOGUS BASIN

Quality: ****
Distance: 13.25 miles
Difficulty: Advanced/expert
Riding time: 2-3 hours
Rating: 1,2,3,4
Season: May-October
Cautions: Yield to other trail users

Getting there: Drive up Bogus Basin Road 13.3 miles from Highlands Elementary School and watch for a 2WD dirt road leading off to the right. Park in the dirt pullout on the right. The ride starts here.

The Ride: This is an excellent escape-the-heat ride in July and August, and an outstanding global tour of the ski area. However, it involves three major climbs that will test the strong riders. To begin, ride out of the pullout and take an immediate right on a 4WD dirt road. This is a service road to the top of Deer Point. At the top of the first little hill, stay left on the main road. Proceed for 2.1 miles to a junction with the Boise Ridge Road. Turn left, hop over the gate, and continue toward Deer Point. Stay on the main road as it bears right and passes under Chair #1. Stay on the two-track as it cruises over to the Showcase lift and descends to the Pine Creek cutoff. Turn right on the cutoff at mile 2.7. Follow the 4WD road as it descends on the backside of the mountain for a mile. Just past the intersection with Nugget, watch for a left-hand turn indicating "easiest way down" at mile 3.8. The sandy road descends on a steep pitch toward the bottom of Chair #6 (Pine Creek). This slippery and eroded 4WD road is tricky. Try to avoid getting pitched. Follow the road behind the chairlift and continue on the two-track, which quickly turns into a singletrack amongst tall grass and it climbs toward the lower slopes below Paradise. The trail get very steep as it turns up a ski run at 5.1 miles. Bear right next to a tall Ponderosa pine tree. The trail hits an even steeper pitch at the base of Goodenough. A new switchback trail may be cut into this slope in the future. At the top of Goodenough, at mile 5.9, turn left and follow the two-track back to the right as it to climbs a mile-long grade to a three-way saddle junction at Majestic. Turn left and head for the top of Shafer Butte, following several switchbacks. After the fourth switchback, you can ride to the summit for a big view or go straight on the Pioneer Lodge traverse. It's two more switchbacks to the top. Continue the tour of Bogus by taking the Pioneer Lodge traverse. Turn left at Morningstar chairlift above the lodge, and follow the road as it dissolves into singletrack and winds down to the lower lodge. Cruise the pavement back to your vehicle at mile 13.2.

Interpretive remarks: Bogus Basin was named for a miner who found pyrite, known as "fool's gold" or "bogus bullion" at the site of the ski area.

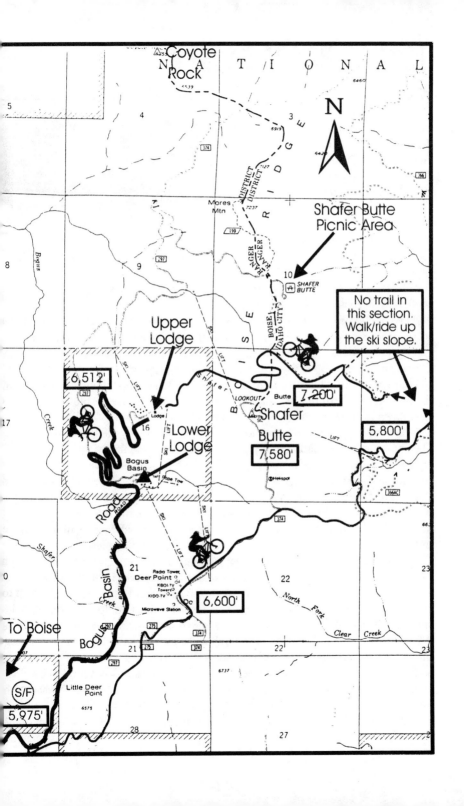

TOUR DE BOGUS BASIN II

Quality: ****
Distance: 8.9 miles
Difficulty: Advanced/expert
Riding time: 2 hours and up
Season: June-October
Cautions: Be prepared to yield to
horseback riders and hikers.

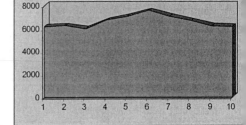

Getting there: Drive up Bogus Basin
Road 16 miles to the Lower Lodge, bear left and proceed to the Bogus Basin Nordic Center parking area, to the left of the road to Pioneer Lodge. Park. The ride starts here.

The Ride: This is an excellent tour of the north and west sides of Bogus Basin, on moderate, steep and gonzo-steep terrain. **To begin,** ride north of the nordic lodge and take an immediate right-hand turn onto a two-track road that climbs behind the lodge. At the top of the first hill, turn hard left and ride around a gate (dirt road on right goes to Bogus Creek Outfitters). The first few miles of the two-track trail are delightful as it rolls up and down along the mountain, parallel with the Ridge Road to your left. At mile 1.3, bear right at the creek crossing, and follow the trail around the bottom of Bitterroot Chairlift. You'll ride through a grassy meadow and then gear down for a gonzo-abusive singletrack climb for one-third of a mile. At mile 1.7, the trail levels out and comes to a three-way junction by the Bogus Creek Outfitters picnic area. Bear left toward the picnic area, and then right as the dirt road peels away from the picnic area, and then right again on a primitive two-track that descends to the bottom of Superior Chairlift. At mile 2.0 bear left on the two-track, and at mile 2.1 bear right at a fork and drop down to the bottom of the lift. Turn right and ride up the draw. A left-turn connects with the Boise Ridge Road if you wish to bail out here. Continuing on, ride up the draw in your small ring. At mile 2.5, the trail switchbacks to the left at the bottom of Nighthawk and Triumph. Get ready for more gonzo-abusive steep climbing on slippery granitic soil for a half mile. At mile 3.1, the two-track merges with a spur that leads to the Shafer Butte Picnic area. Bear right and climb toward the top of Shafer Buttle. At mile 3.3, bear right and climb. At mile 3.6, bear right at switchback junction. Ignore a left-hand spur at mile 3.7 and ride across the face of Superior on the Pioneer traverse. At mile 3.9, turn hard left and make the final climb to the top of Shafer Butte (7,600 feet) at mile 4.9. Take a moment to soak in the view. Ride over to the top of Superior Chair, and pick up a singletrack heading west, to the north of the rocky crags. Follow this singletrack as it snakes through a number of tight switchbacks and steep descents to the Pioneer Traverse (mile 5.8). Turn left and cruise to the top of Morning Star Chairlift. Turn left and follow Sunshine, or the wildflower trail, to the bottom of the Showcase Chairlift (mile 7.8). Bear left, ride past the lower lodge to your vehicle.

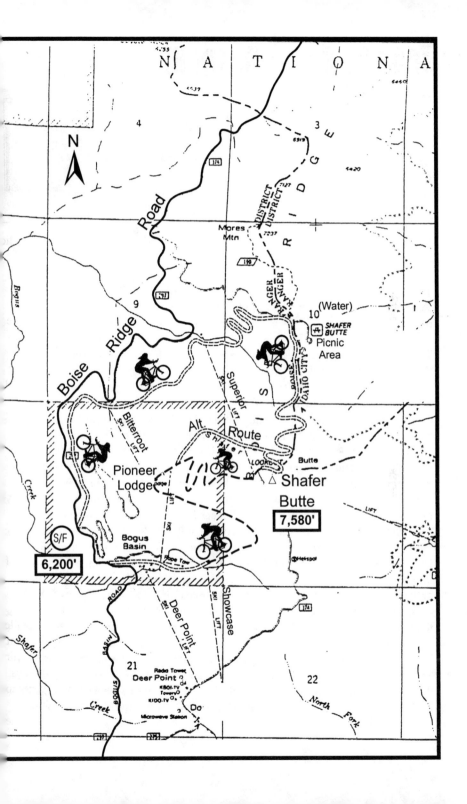

TOUR DE BOGUS BASIN III

Quality: ****
Distance: 8.7 miles
Difficulty: Advanced/expert
Riding time: 1.5 hours and up
Season: June-October
Cautions: Be prepared to yield to
horseback riders and hikers.

Getting there: Drive up Bogus Basin
Road 16 miles to the Lower Lodge.
Park. The ride starts here.

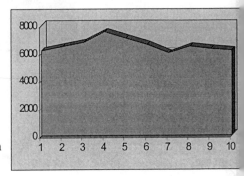

The Ride: This is an excellent tour of three sides of Bogus Basin, on moderate, steep and gonzo-steep terrain. Don't let the mileage trick you -- there are a couple of abusive singletrack climbs in this loop that will test strong riders.

To begin, ride from the lower lodge up the gully to the east to the bottom of the Showcase Chairlift (mile.7). As you approach the bottom of the lift, look for a singletrack trail taking off behind the lift hut. Ride up the singletrack as it climbs into tall grass, brush and thick wildflowers. Hang on, it gets steep. After the trail switchbacks, the climbing gets a little easier. At mile 1.6, you reach an initial saddle above the Pioneer Lodge next to Morning Star chairlift. Turn right and follow the Pioneer Traverse toward the top of Bogus Basin. At mile 2.1, you'll reach a switchback junction. Follow the singletrack uphill and climb a couple switchbacks to the top of Shafer Butte (mile 3.1). Take a breather and enjoy the view. Now you're going to descend the switchbacks to the south to Shafer Butte picnic area. At mile 4.1, turn right at the sign for the Pioneer Lodge and continue on the switchback descent to the picnic area. At mile 4.9, turn left on a primitive two-track, going downhill, right before you reach the picnic area. This will take you down several steep switchbacks to the bottom of the Superior chairlift (mile 5.9). Take an immediate left at the bottom of the lift and climb the grassy two-track up a steep grade. You're riding on a ski traverse that climbs for a half mile. At mile 6.0 bear right on a two-track and climb. At mile 6.4, bear left and then right and you'll come to a big clearing with picnic benches set up by Bogus Creek Outfitters. Bear right as you ride past the picnic area, and cruise over to the bottom of the Bitterroot Chairlift (mile 6.8). Bear left on the two-track (don't go out on the main dirt road) and follow it as it wraps around the mountain, running parallel above the ridge road. At mile 8.1, ride around the gate and take a hard right to exit the trail onto the Boise Ridge Road and the Bogus Basin Nordic Lodge. Turn left and head back to your vehicle by the lower lodge (mile 8.7)

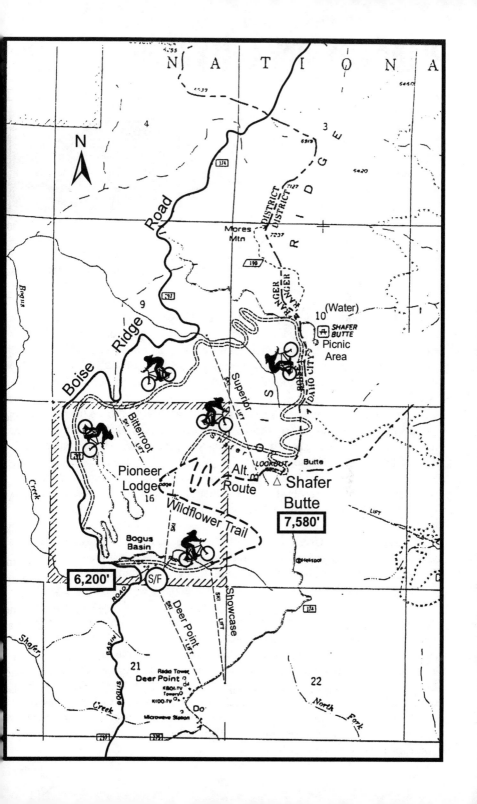

HARD GUY-DRY CREEK LOOP

Quality: ****
Distance: 22 miles
Difficulty: Expert
Riding time: 4-6 hours
Trail: Two-track, single-track
Season: June-early October
Trail also open to: Walkers, runners, equestrians

Getting there: Ride or drive to Highlands School, at the intersection of Bogus Basin Road and Curling Drive. Park in the school parking lot. The ride starts here.

The Ride: It's a tough climb up Hard Guy Trail, but the Dry Creek trail provides a rich reward. For experts, this loop combo is one of the highest quality rides in the Boise Foothills. The ride takes you from the hot and dry open foothills landscape into a shady, densely forest creek-bottom that's chock full of wildlife. This is a long, arduous ride, so bring lots of food and water.

To begin, ride up Bogus Basin 1.8 miles to the Corrals Trail #31 on the right. Take Corrals to the Hard Guy junction on the left at mile 3.2. Climb Hard Guy #33 to the top -- it's 5 miles of gut-wrenching climbing to the Boise Ridge Road (mile 8.3). Turn left and ride 3 miles to the Dry Creek junction at 11.3. (Cyclists also can approach Dry Creek from Bogus Basin Road to the west, or you can climb up 8th Street instead of climbing Hard Guy. It's about four miles from the 8th Street junction with the Ridge Road to the Dry Creek turnoff).

To descend into Dry Creek, turn left off the ridge road on a singletrack trail. It wraps around a ridge and hairpins into the densely timbered headwaters of Dry Creek. Proceed with caution. The trail follows a very loose surface on a steep descent for the first mile or so. Then, you'll get into an area of multiple creek crossings after mile 12. High water in the spring of 1997 made many of the upper crossings deep and difficult to ride. Take time to enjoy the lovely forested trail, beaver ponds and wildlife. At mile 13.8, the trail emerges into an opening; a nice lunch spot. At mile 15.5, the Shingle Creek trail comes in from the left. At mile 16.1, there will be a left-hand spur that goes back to Hard Guy and Corrals. Note the junction for future reference. Continuing down Dry Creek, the trail becomes more technical as it winds through granite mini-spires and boulders. Use caution. You'll hit Bogus Basin Road at 17.7 miles. Now it's 4 miles back to the school, mostly downhill, on the pavement. Now it's time to hunt for a hot tub and relax -- you earned it.

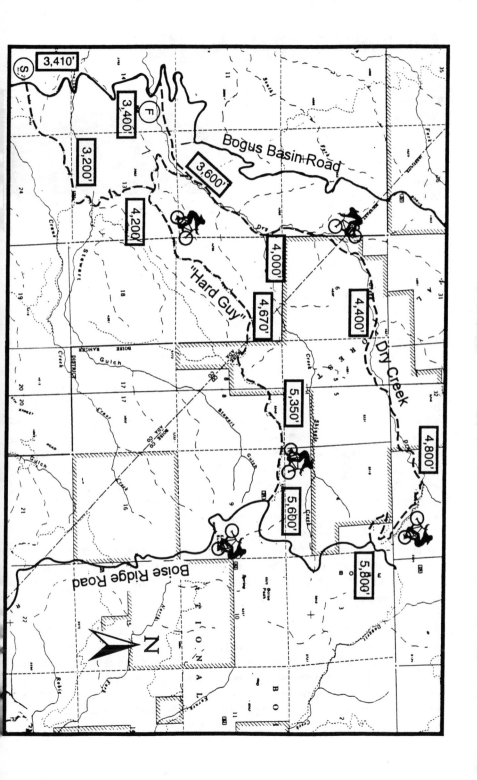

SIDEWINDER-TRAIL #4 LOOP

Quality: ***
Distance: 5.4 miles
Difficulty: Advanced
Riding time: 30 minutes-
1.5 hours
Trail: Single track
Season: April-October
Watch out for: Hikers, joggers
and downhill cyclists

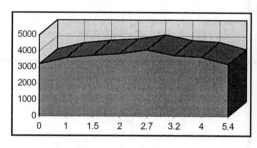

Getting there: Mileage for this ride starts from the Crestline trailhead. To reach the trailhead, cruise up 8th Street in Boise's North End to Brumback Street. Turn right and climb the paved street as it turns into Boise Hills Drive and then Crestline Drive to a dirt parking lot on the right. You also could ride Red Fox Trail from Camel's Back and climb Kestrel to Crestline to add more dirt to the ride.

The Ride: This loop ride is one notch more difficult than the Crestline-Hulls loop in the respect that it features more difficult climbing and a steep, technical descent. This is why this ride is rated advanced. Strong intermediates may want to try this ride to improve endurance and downhill riding skills. Sidewinder Trail #24 was built by SWIMBA volunteers in the fall of 1995, and it was laid out by Tim Breuer, the Ridge to Rivers trail coordinator. It was the first major new trail that SWIMBA volunteers built in the Boise Foothills. The success of that project paved the way for subsequent new trails to be built in the Boise Front. **To begin,** head up Crestline Trail #28 for 1.3 miles to the Sidewinder (Trail #24) junction. The trailhead is marked by a brown carcinite sign. Turn right and begin a gradual but steady climb on Sidewinder. The trail gets steeper as you climb. At mile 2.1, the trail gets granny-gear steep for a bit, and then you'll come to a saddle junction with Trail #4 at mile 2.7. Take a breather and soak up the view. Be ready for a technical descent on Trail #4. The trail can get rutted and v-trenched at times where it tries to suck your front wheel into a rut and cause you to crash. It's rideable most of the time for advanced riders. It's a half-mile descent back to the Crestline Trail. Turn left to return to the trailhead at mile 5.4.

Variations: Instead of descending on Trail #4 at the Sidewinder Junction, climb Trail #4 to the junction with Trail #5, and descend on the Trail #5 ridge over to Shane's Trail and Rocky Canyon Road. This is a longer loop that experts will enjoy. See page 90 for a complete description of the Trail #4, Trail #5 and Trail #6 network. Another alternative would be to descend to the Crestline-Trail #4 junction, turn right, climb to the motorcycle parking lot on 8th Street, and take Trail #1 over to Bob's Trail #30 for a final descent into town.

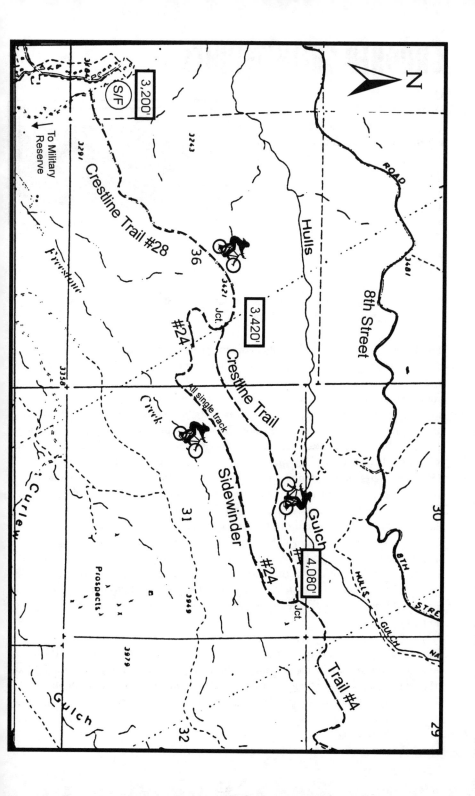

CROOKED SUMMIT-PINES

Quality: ****
Distance: 22 miles
Difficulty: Advanced-Expert
Riding time: 3.5-5 hours
Trail: Major dirt road, two-track, singletrack
Season: May-October
Trail also open to: Runners, walkers, equestrians, motorcycles, 4WD. Please yield to all trail users. Uphill traffic has the right of way!

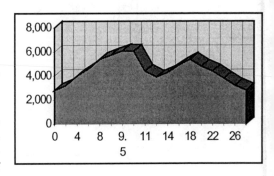

Getting there: Ride or drive about 3.5 miles up 8th Street to the motorcycle parking lot. Park. The ride starts here.

The Ride: This ride is a hill-climbers dream. It's not a technical ride, but an excellent training run that provides a peek into the backside of the Boise Front. If you're wondering whether you've got the legs or lungs for this route, ask yourself if you can ride from town to the Boise Ridge (3,250 vertical feet) and then have something left for a second, 1,600-vertical-foot climb. If bold intermediate riders give themselves enough time, this route could be doable with several rests. Begin the climb by riding up 8th Street to the Boise Ridge Road. It's a tedious, predictable 8.5-mile ride up a steep ridge spine. Once you reach the ridge, turn left and climb 250 more "verts" to Eagleson Summit (mile 5.9). At the big three-way junction, turn right and head for Crooked Summit. After a short climb, the road plunges 2,000 "verts" over four miles on a delightfully swoopy two-track road. At Crooked Summit (mile 11), descend down the larger dirt road past the tarpaper shacks of the Karney Lakes subdivision. Watch for the dog at mile 12.2 and then at 12.6, turn right to the Pines Tavern. If it's open, by all means, have a hamburger and fries and lounge on the deck before tackling the 1,600-foot climb back to the Boise Ridge. On this route to the ridge, there are a number of private inholdings on both sides of the trail. Please respect private property, and observe no trespassing, no hunting and no fishing signs.

Once you're back on the Boise Ridge Road, you've got a ton of options. But if you drove your rig to the motorcycle parking lot, you'll have to head back via Trail #4 (see page 90) or 8th Street. Or, riders could descend to Aldape Summit and Rocky Canyon Road or take Trail #7 down to Rocky Canyon Road.

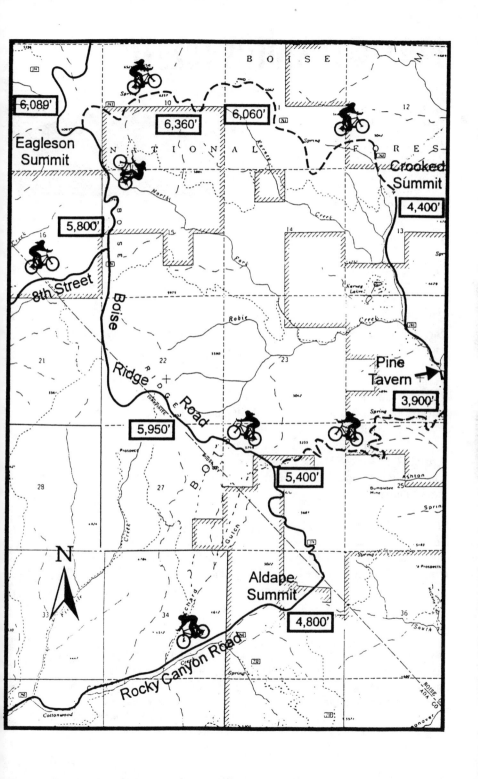

8TH STREET-SCOTT'S-CORRALS

Quality: ***
Distance: 10 miles
Difficulty: Intermediate
Riding time: 1.5-3 hours
Trail: Major dirt road; two-track, singletrack.
Season: April-October
Trails also open to: Runners, walkers, horseback riders, motorcycles; please yield to all trail users.

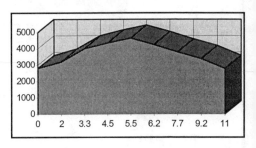

Getting there: Ride up 8th Street, past the North End, into the foothills. Mileage is clocked from the BLM sign located near the first left-hand bend in the road.

The Ride: The following descriptions offer several options off to the left side of 8th Street. For one reason or another, mountain bikers seem to concentrate on the right side of 8th Street, so it's a refreshing change to try these left-side loops. **To begin,** cruise up 8th Street or Hulls Gulch to the motorcycle parking lot (3 miles; add .3 for Hulls Gulch). Directly across from the parking lot, Trail #1 takes off toward the Corrals Trail and Bob's Trail. You're now about to ride the Corrals-Trail #1 loop backwards, which is much more difficult than riding it the other way. Follow Trail #1 on a downhill grade to the junction of Bob's, and then climb up Trail #31 to the Corral's summit. Now you've earned a fun, three-mile downhill descent on the Corrals Trail back to Bogus Basin Road. Watch out for riders, walkers and joggers coming up the Corrals Trail. Finish the loop by heading down Bogus Basin Road back to town.

To reach Scott's Trail, ride from the motorcycle parking lot 2.4 miles to the junction with Scott's, Trail #32. It's a fairly steep, arduous climb from the parking lot to Scott's so spin and conserve energy. Scott's Trail features a fairly steep single-track descent to the high saddle on the Corrals route (mile 6.1). Take your time and feather your brakes to avoid skidding. From the Corrals saddle, you can turn right and cruise downhill for three miles to Bogus Basin Road, or turn left and head back to 8th Street and Bob's Trail on Trail #31. You make the call.

Interpretive note: Scott's Trail is named for Scott Van Kleek, a Boise native and longtime mountain biker. The story goes that Scott was one of the first cyclists to try Scott's trail instead of the upper Hulls Gulch Nature Trail, which used to be open to mountain biking in the early 1980s. In those days, only a few people were into mountain biking, and if you saw another rider, you usually knew who they were. Scott's Trail was developed initially as an old horse and livestock trail.

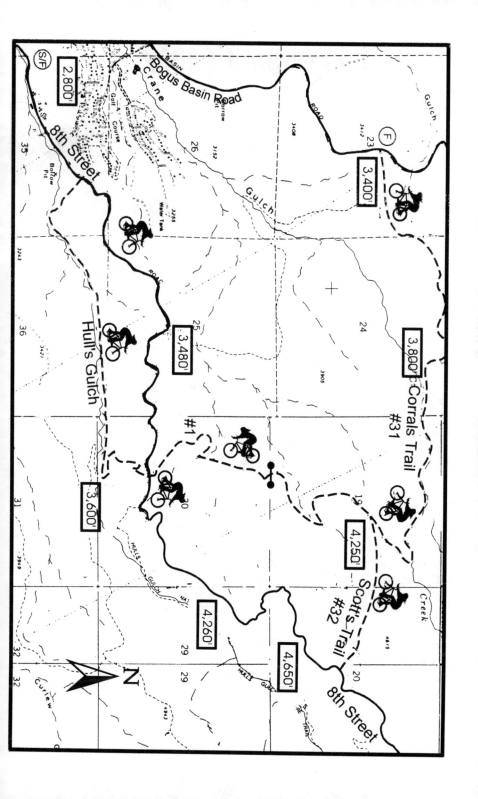

THREE BEARS-SHANE'S LOOP

Quality: ***
Distance: 6.6 miles
Difficulty: Advanced/expert
Riding time: 1-2 hours
Trail: Dirt road, two-track, singletrack
Season: April-October
Watch out for: Horses, mountain bikers, runners, hikers

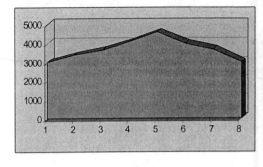

Getting there: Ride or drive from Fort Boise to the end of the pavement on Rocky Canyon Road. Take Reserve Street north to Shaw Mountain Road, bear right and follow Shaw Mountain to the junction with Table Rock Road. Bear left and follow Rocky Canyon Road about 1 mile to the end of the pavement. The ride starts here.

The Ride: This is a relatively new ride in the Boise Foothills. It's fairly short, mileage- and timewise, so it's a good option for advanced and expert riders when they don't have time for a longer ride. Strong intermediate riders could try this ride, realizing that several super-steep climbing sections may have to be walked.

To begin, cruise up Rocky Canyon Road about 2.3 miles to a sharp left-hand hairpin turn at a gated trailhead. The beginning of Three Bears is past the cattleguard (mile 1.7), and before the Five Mile Creek trailhead (mile 2.5).

Climb the initial switchback in your small ring and conserve energy for a steeper climb coming up at mile 2.5. Now it's a granny gear climb up a steep slope that falls away at a weird cant. Try to maintain your line and continue climbing toward the saddle of Curlew Ridge. You will see a left-hand arrow sign at mile 2.8. Bear left and follow the switchback trail as it winds to the left, and then to the right, before it heads for the Curlew Ridge saddle at mile 3.26. Take a moment to enjoy the view and look for hawks. The trail to the right is closed; it lies on private land. Go left and head down the ridge to Shane's Trail #26A (mile 5.19). During the steep descent, watch out for mobile rocks ("death cookies"), sand and small v-shaped gullies on the trail that can eat the front tire and send you sailing over the handlebars.

At the junction with Shane's Trail, you can turn left and head directly for Rocky Canyon Road, or you can turn right and take the lower loop back to Rocky Canyon or to Trail #26 and Trail #5. Going left, it's just under a mile to Rocky Canyon Road (mile 6). You reach the pavement at mile 6.6.

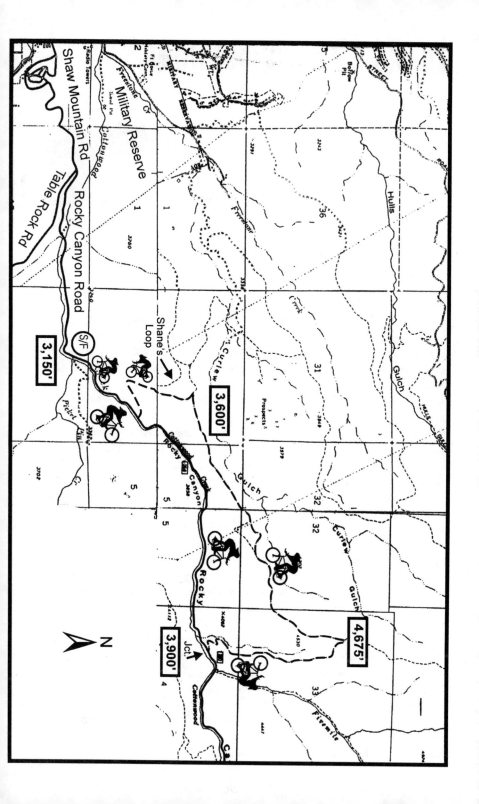

TRAILS 4-5-6 "RIDGE ROMP"

Quality: ****
Distance: 18-20 miles
Difficulty: Advanced-Expert
Riding time: 3-6 hours
Trail: Two-track, singletrack
Season: April-October
Watch out for: Motorcycles, steep
drops, equestrians, cars and trucks.

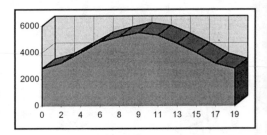

Getting there: Take either Rocky
Canyon Road or 8th Street to the Boise Ridge Road and the Trail #4 junction. The
Trail #4 junction on the Boise Ridge Road is 3.4 miles northwest from Aldape
Summit, and 1 mile from 8th Street (via the singletrack connector trail). It's usually
signed.

The Ride: Once you've exerted the effort to climb to the Boise Ridge, you deserve
a big reward. In this case, you get to revel in a huge ridge romp, one that seems to
last forever. You can look forward to dropping 3,000 vertical feet, and along the
way, you've got three options — you guessed it — Trails #4, #5 or #6. Start on
Trail #4, also known as "Devil's Slide" and "Dave's Trail." From the ridge road, it
descends over some whoop-de-doos and then follows a ridge spine to a junction
with Trail #6 at 1.4 miles. Trail #6 features some nasty steep climbs -- some too
steep to ride -- and it tours a southwest finger-ridge and then links up with Trail #5.
You must stay with Trail #4 if you plan to end up on Crestline, Hulls Gulch or 8th
Street. Continue on Trail #4 and watch out for the rocky, eroded steep drops. Either
get way back over your back tire in the "hemorrhoid-polishing" position and try to
make the descents or walk. It's 1.8 miles to the junction with Trail #5. Remain on
Trail #4, and drop another four miles to the intersection with the Crestline Trail.
From here, you can drop down Crestline, ride over to Hulls or 8th Street.

From the Trail #6 junction, the two-track road drops for 1.5 miles to a small draw.
The trail is steep, soft and rutted in places, requiring advanced downhill riding
skills. Once in the draw, you must climb a singletrack to the junction with Trail #5.
This is a 2.8-mile side trip.

Trail #5 peels off from Trail #4 about 2.7 miles from the ridge road. It's a nice
alternative because the trail has turned into singletrack, it's less technical than Trail
#4, it's not open to motorcycles and it doesn't receive as much use overall. Trail #5
dumps out on a private driveway, on which an easement has been obtained, called
Trail #26. Turn left on the road and follow the signs for Trail #26, as it turns into a
cool singletrack and winds over to Shane's Trail, #26A. At the junction with
Shane's, turn left and climb a half mile to a small summit, and then it's downhill all
the way to Rocky Canyon Road. Wa-hoo!

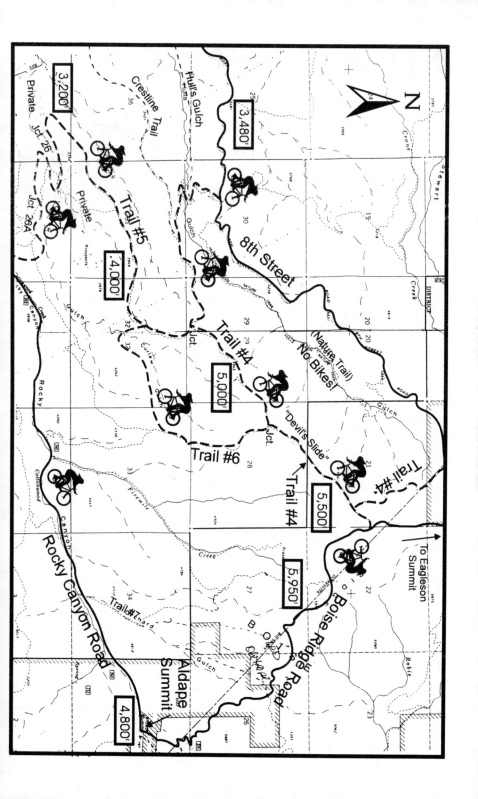

R. CANYON-TRAIL#7 LOOP

Quality: ***
Distance: 18.3 miles
Difficulty: Advanced-expert
Riding time: 2.5-4 hours
Trail: 2WD road, 4WD road, singletrack
Season: May-October
Watch out for: Vehicles, washboard ruts, loose pea-gravel.

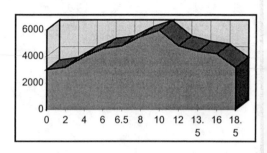

Getting there: Go north on Reserve Street (parallel to Fort Boise) and turn right onto Shaw Mountain Road. It's two miles to a junction with Shaw Mountain Road and Table Rock Road. Veer left to Rocky Canyon Road. Mileage for the ride starts here.

The Ride: The Rocky Canyon Road-Aldape Summit-Trail #7 loop is another excellent, but challenging training ride. It features a 6.5-mile climb up Rocky Canyon Road to Aldape Summit, and then another steep 3.3-mile climb to the Trail #7 turnoff on the Boise Ridge Road. Then it's a fun descent into Orchard Gulch, and riders will enjoy the expansive views of the east side of the Boise Front and several old mines. As you're riding up Rocky Canyon Road, you'll note the Trail #7 junction on the left at 5.2 miles, about a mile or so from the summit. This is where you'll drop out on the road after riding the loop. At Aldape Summit (mile 6.5), turn left on the Boise Ridge Road and climb toward tree line. The road is quite steep at the outset, particularly in the first mile or so. But stay with it, the road gradient will taper off. Ignore several trails peeling off the ridge road to the left. None of the singletrack routes continue to the bottom. I know, I checked them out. Avoid the big wide-track dirt road that plunges down a ridge to Rocky Canyon. The BLM has closed this highly eroded route; and they plan to reseed it. At mile 9.5, the road flattens out and it may be possible to ride in your middle ring. The Trail #7 turnoff is on the left at mile 9.8. Trail #7 descends at a brisk pace. Keep your speed down; the road surface is loose, pink pea-sized gravel. The trail drops quickly out of the trees and then contours down to a saddle above Five-Mile Creek at about mile 11.5. Stay on the main trail and descend into Orchard Gulch, a lush and beautiful riparian area. It's another 1.6 miles to Rocky Canyon Road. You may want to take a break while you can enjoy the shade provided by cottonwood trees in the draw. You'll reach Rocky Canyon Road at 13.1 miles. Now it's 5.2 miles back to the start.

Variations: Reverse the loop and try climbing Trail #7 to the ridge road. It's a real gut-buster, especially with the loose surface in the upper section, but it's good practice for riders who revel in self-inflicted punishment.

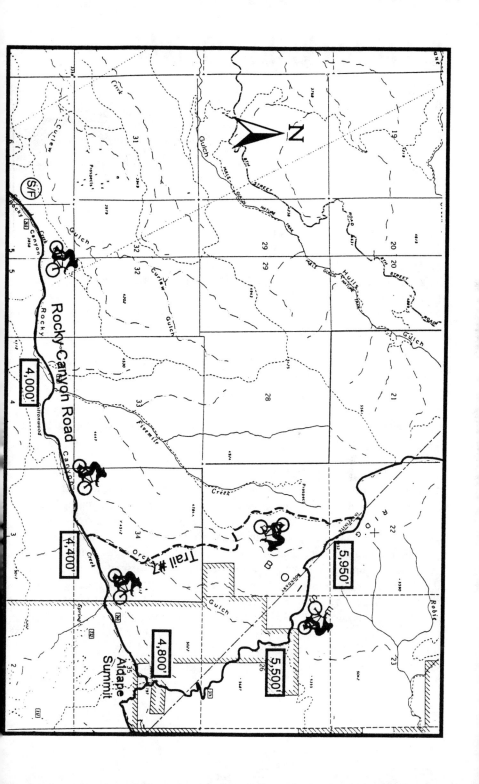

R. CANYON RIGHT-SIDE LOOP

Quality: ***
Distance: 12.6 miles
Difficulty: Advanced
Riding time: 1.5-3 hours
Rating: 2WD road, 4WD road, singletrack
Season: May-October
Topo map: Robie Creek

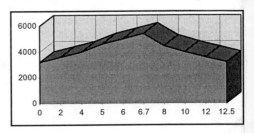

Getting there: Mileage for this loop ride starts and finishes at the end of the pavement parking area at the foot of Rocky Canyon. To reach this point, head for Fort Boise Park on the east side of town, at the intersection of Fort Street and Reserve Street. Follow Reserve Street in a northerly direction to the edge of the foothills. Bear right on Shaw Mountain Road to the top of the hill. Watch for the junction of Table Rock and Shaw Mountain roads, and bear left on Shaw Mountain. Now you're on Rocky Canyon Road. The pavement ends in 1.4 miles.

The Ride: The Rocky Canyon Right-Side Loop is a shorter alternative to riding over the top of Shaw Mountain, and it adds a little zest to an up-and-back ride to Aldape Summit. The trail isn't very obvious at the beginning, so many riders probably haven't seen it or tried it before. Caution: Portions of this trail lie on private land, but it is not posted. Please tread lightly. The use of this trail could change in the future.

To begin, head up Rocky Canyon Road. Conserve energy and spin a comfortable climbing gear because this ride involves a longer climb than the ride to Aldape Summit. Watch out for vehicles speeding up or down the road, it's getting busier all the time. At mile 5.0, you'll come to a major road peeling off to the right — this is your turnoff to reach the right-side loop trail. On BLM maps, the route is called Trail E. The turn is about a quarter-mile before the top of Aldape Summit. At press time, the trail junction was marked with a beat-up brown carsonite sign. Proceed up the narrow but smooth dirt road for 1.7 miles to a singletrack trail peeling off to the right. The slippery trail weaves down into the next draw, following several switchbacks. At mile 7.8, you'll come to a junction. Turn right to complete the loop back to Rocky Canyon Road, or turn left if you want to climb back up to Trail E. At mile 8.1, the trail dumps out on Rocky Canyon Road. It's 4.5 miles back to the end of the pavement.

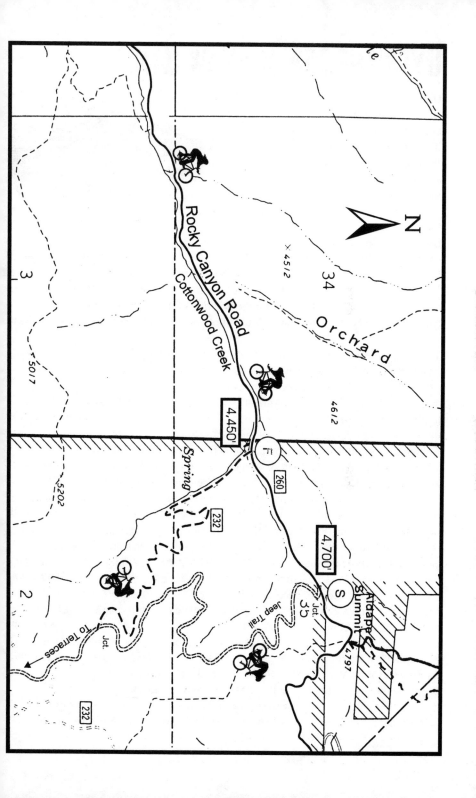

OVER THE TOP OF SHAW MTN.

Quality: ****
Distance: 20 miles and up
Difficulty: Advanced/Expert
Riding time: 2-5 hours
Rating: 2WD road, 4WD road, single-track
Season: May-October

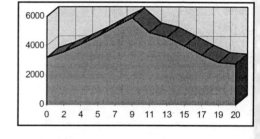

Getting there: Mileage for this ride starts at the end-of-the-pavement parking area at the foot of Rocky Canyon. To reach this point, head for Fort Boise Park in east Boise, at the intersection of Fort Street and Reserve Street. Follow Reserve Street in a northerly direction to the edge of the foothills. Bear right on Shaw Mountain Road. Watch for the junction of Table Rock and Shaw Mountain roads, and bear left on Shaw Mountain. Now you're on Rocky Canyon Road.

The Ride: The ride over the top of Shaw Mountain involves some arduous long-distance climbing, but it's worth the pain to enjoy big 360-degree views from the top of the mountain at 5,900 feet. Once on top, you'll have a number of downhill options, including Trail E to Highland Valley, Trail #8 to Squaw Creek or the trail to the Adelmann Mine.

To begin, spin up Rocky Canyon Road 5.0 miles to a major dirt road on the right. The turn is a quarter-mile short of Aldape Summit. Turn right and spin up the road, known as Trail E. Conserve energy because there are some major steeps ahead. You'll notice the road climbs into the timber zone, providing much-needed shade in the hot summer months. At mile 6.5, the road gets a little steeper as it climbs to a four-way saddle junction at mile 7.0. Bear right at this junction and stay on Trail E, bypassing three roads to your left. Get ready for a series of steep granny-gear climbs for the final ascent. At mile 7.7, you'll crest the first summit. Take a breather and munch some food. The junction for the Terraces trail comes up about 50 yards on the right for future reference. Go straight on Trail E. The junction for Trail #8 comes up at mile 8.2. Turn right if you want to take this very rough two-track down to Squaw Creek. Continue on Trail E to a T-junction at mile 8.6. Bear left to stay with Trail E. Now you can enjoy a major descent, heading for Highland Valley Summit. Take a left on Trail #9 (a singletrack trail) at mile 10.2 if you wish to tour the Black Hornet Mine. It's a cool side-trip and a nice trail. Back on Trail E, it descends three more miles to a T-junction with Highland Valley Road. Trail #11 goes to the right, which exits across from the Crow Inn. Going left on Trail F takes you to Idaho 21, above Lucky Peak. Turn right and head back to Boise.

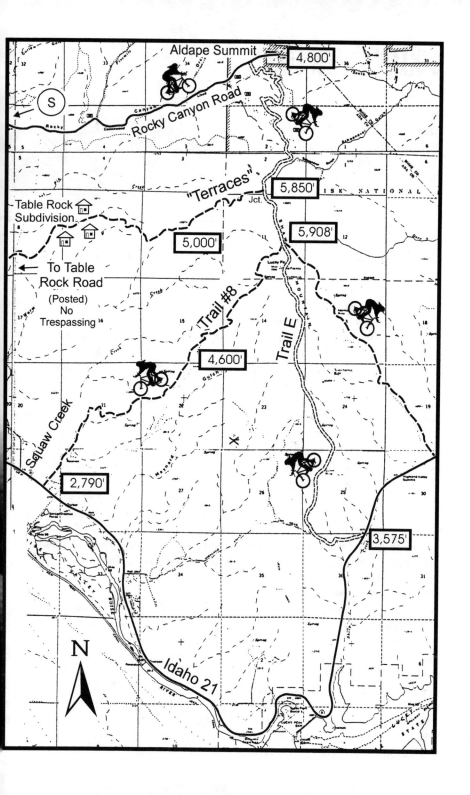

SQUAW CREEK LOOPS

Quality: ***
Distance: 9.9- miles and up
Difficulty: Advanced
Riding time: 1-1.5 hours
Trail: Singletrack, two-track
Season: April-October
Special note: Please observe winter closure for wintering deer.
Getting there: Head east on the Greenbelt, past Eckert Road, to Council Springs Road. Turn left and ride straight for the foothills to a Fish and Game gate (5 miles from Municipal Park). The ride starts here.

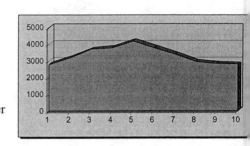

The Ride: The Squaw Creek-Crow Inn Loops provide a nifty bird's-eye view of the old Barber Valley and a wildlife tour. The trails in this area pass through the Boise River Wildlife Management Area, owned by the Idaho Department of Fish and Game. A seasonal wildlife closure occurs each year from Nov. 1-April 15. Approximately 3,000 mule deer winter in the Boise Foothills. Please give deer herds a wide berth. Be ready for some steep climbing ... **To begin** the ride, hoist your bike over the gate and proceed up the two-track road. After climbing for .4 miles, shift into low gear for the first of seven major hills in this route. Ignore the junction on left at .7 miles. Keep climbing. After the fifth hill, you'll arrive at a saddle junction with Trail #8 at mile 2.2. Go right, and enjoy a fast downhill and some rolling terrain until you climb again. At mile 3.6, Trail #13, a singletrack, peels off to the right and descends to Idaho 21, west of the Crow Inn. For a longer workout, stay on the main trail and climb a bit more, until the two-track evens out and begins to descend at a fast pace. At mile 4.9, pass by the junction with Trail E and keep riding downhill. At mile 5.5, peel off on the singletrack trail and descend on Trail #11 for a really fun ripping descent to the trailhead at the end of Highland Valley Road (mile 7.3). Ride out to Warm Springs Avenue, turn right to the Crow Inn parking lot, go left into the southeast corner of the lot and drop down to the Greenbelt to return to the Squaw Creek trailhead (mile 9.9).

Variation #1: Climb Squaw Creek to the junction with Trail #11, keep going, and turn left on Trail E (mile 4.9), to climb four miles to the top of Lucky Peak (elevation 5,908). This route is not as steep as Trail 8, but it's close. After you reach the top, follow Trail E over the top of Shaw Mountain to Rocky Canyon Road, turn left, and descend back to Boise. Distance: 24 miles.

Variation #2: Go left at mile 2.1 and climb Trail #8 to Lucky Peak and Shaw Mountain. This route is rough and grueling. At the top of Trail #8, turn right and climb to the top of Lucky Peak. Bear left at the top, and descend on Trail E and then Trail #11 to the Crow Inn. Return to Squaw Creek Trailhead. Distance: 20 miles.

Variation #3: See Tom Platt's favorite foothills singletrack, page 110.

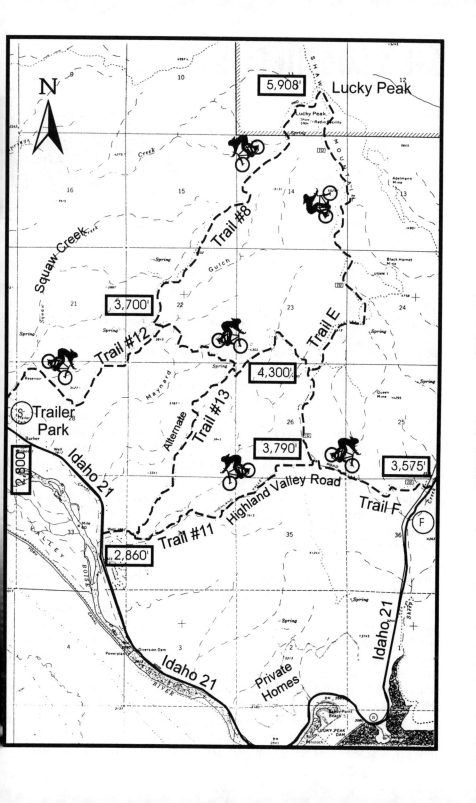

KEN'S FAVORITE EVENING RIDE

Quality: ****
Distance: 11.6 miles
Difficulty: Strong intermediate. Riders will encounter short, steep climbs and technical descents that can be walked.
Riding time: 1-1.5 hours
Trail: Singletrack, two-track
Season: Spring to fall

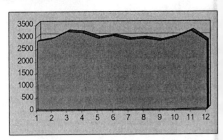

Ken Snider

Getting there:
Ride or drive to the trailhead in the northeast end of Camel's Back Park. The ride starts here.

The Ride: This is one of Ken's favorite weeknight rides in the Boise Foothills. It features three loops in Military Reserve. He typically meets up with some friends to do the ride, and they go to Lucky 13 afterward. "I like the ride because it has a lot of ups and downs," Ken says. "It's kind of like interval training." **To begin,** ride to the junction of Red Fox and Hulls Pond trails. Go right on Hulls Pond, and follow the two-track to the north. At mile .5, cross a parking lot and 8th Street and pick up Owl's Roost, still riding north. At mile 1.2, turn right on Kestrel and ride to Crestline. Turn right on Crestline, and then take a left on the Military Reserve Connector Trail #23. Follow the Connector trail to the sandy driveway and Mountain Cove Road (mile 2.7). Turn right on the dirt road and then turn left by the parking lot on Central Ridge Trail #22. Climb #22 to the Central Ridge, turn right and descend to the switchbacks (mile 3.6). Go straight on #22A, then left on Freestone Creek Trail #22B. Follow the trail to the main trailhead at mile 3.8. Turn left and ride up the Toll Road Trail #27A to the Eagle Ridge junction at mile 4.3. Turn right and follow Eagle Ridge Trail #25 to the top of the ridge. At mile 4.7, bear right on Eagle Ridge Loop Trail #25A. Follow the loop trail around the knoll, cross the pavement and follow the singletrack to the top of the rock pinnacle, and then go right and follow the Ponds Loop Trail #21 down to the dog play areas. At the bottom of the hill (mile 5.7), turn right and follow the gravel road next to the mountain toward the main trailhead. At mile 5.8, take the low road. As the road dissolves to singletrack and then dumps out on the concrete apron, turn left and ride/walk over to the paved road, turn right and go back to the main trailhead (mile 6.3). Go straight, up #27A, to the Eagle Ridge junction. Turn right, and follow the trail around to the Cottonwood Creek Trail #27. Follow #27 toward the Black Forest. At mile 7.4, bend to the left and follow signs for #27. You'll emerge from the Black Forest by the concrete apron at mile 7.8. Take an immediate right, go back to the main trailhead. Go left on Freestone Creek Trail #22B, and follow the singletrack to the Central Ridge. At mile 8.4, bear left to the parking lot and retrace your tread to Camel's Back Park.

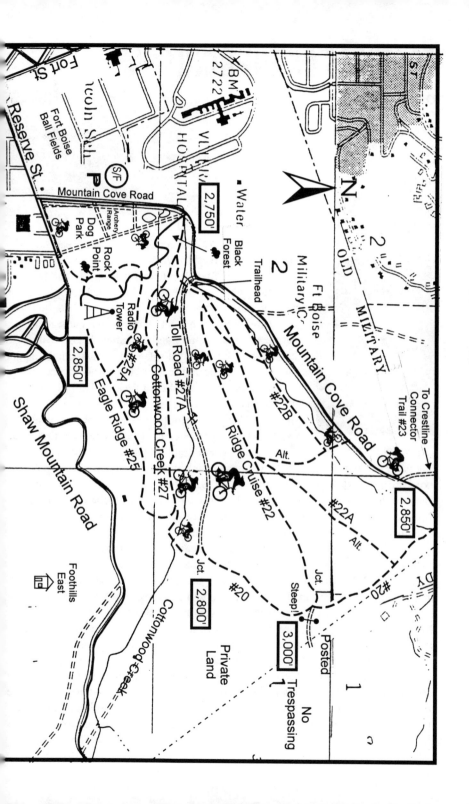

FOOTHILLS ON THE ROCKS

Quality: ****
Distance: 5.3 miles
Difficulty: Strong intermediate; Riders will encounter several steep climbs and technical stair-step drops that can be walked.
Riding time: 45 minutes to 1 hour
Trail: Singletrack, two-track
Season: Spring to fall

Tim Breuer

Getting there: Take Warm Springs Avenue east of Broadway, past the M&W Market, to a signed left-hand turn for the Old State Penitentiary. Turn left, and follow signs to a public parking area behind the Bishop's House. The ride starts here.

The Ride: For this concoction, mix equal parts geology, Native American history and settlement history with a dash of technical riding, a splash of vertical climbing, and a jigger of solitude and scenery that'll knock your socks off. Shake don't stir. **To begin,** pick up Trail #15 and climb on Trail #19 to the top of Castle Rock, a rock pinnacle. This point affords great views of the Boise Valley. At the top, turn right on Trail #18 and climb the Castle Rock Quarry Trail. Watch for the first right-hand junction at mile .8. Take it. You will encounter a steep, stair-step rocky drop. Some experts can ride it. Most people choose not to. Follow the trail back to the main Table Rock Trail #15 (mile 1.0) and climb up the South Face to the top of Table Rock (elevation 3,650'). Pause midway up to read about the geologic history of the area provided by the Geological Museum (mile 2.0). It's a good excuse to rest. Near the top of Table Rock, at mile 2.2, instead of heading for the cross, follow a two-track across a grassy flat toward Table Rock Road. Look for a gate by the entrance to the Table Rock Quarry. To the left of the gate, pick up Trail #16, a singletrack, and ride along the east rim. The next stretch will make you feel a million miles from downtown, with excellent stands of native grasses and shrubs. Listen for the descending call of canyon wrens. At mile 2.7, follow the trail sign and take a hard hairpin turn to the left, thereby avoiding the rock quarry. Turn right at a saddle, and drop down toward the Warm Springs Mesa housing development. Go over the gate. Then, take each right-hand turn that comes your way. You'll pass by the location of an old tramway, where prison inmates hauled sandstone rocks from the quarry to the valley floor. At mile 3.6, turn right on a steep uphill singletrack and climb. At mile 3.8, turn right again and follow Trail #16 under the powerline corridor back to Trail #15. Return to the Old Pen parking area. End mileage: 5.3. -- Tim Breuer

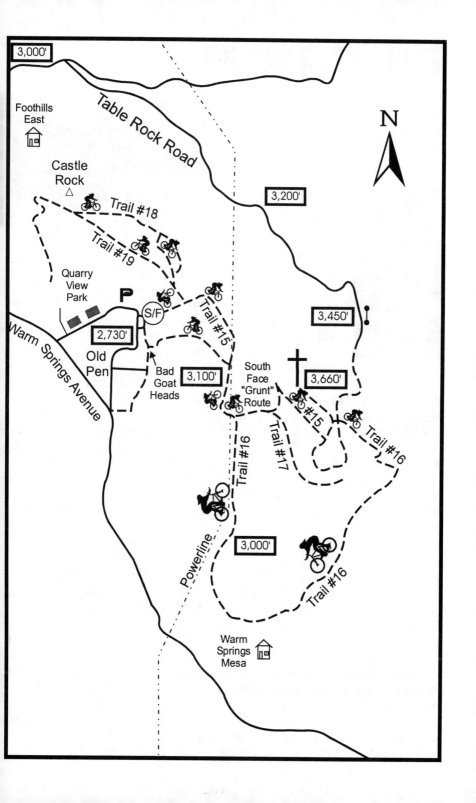

BOMB SQUAD BRUISER

Quality: ****
Distance: 14.5 miles
Difficulty: Advanced
Riding time: 1.5-2 hours
Trail: Singletrack, two-track
Season: Spring to fall

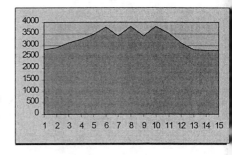

Getting there: Ride or drive to Camel's Back Park. The ride starts here.

The Ride: Jenny Hennessy, founder of the Boise Off-Road Mountain Bike Babes (the BOMB Squad) shared this route as one of many circuits that her group rides in the Boise Foothills. She calls it the Bomb Squad Bruiser because it features several bruising elements that will scorch your lungs and make your thighs burn.

Jenny

To begin, head over to the east side of Camel's Back Park, past the tennis courts, and pick up the singletrack trail near the 9th Street trailhead. Ride north on the Red Fox trail, past the Hulls Gulch ponds and head for the big water tank ahead. At mile .6, turn right on Chickadee Ridge Loop and follow the trail until it dumps out on Red Fox, next to 8th Street (mile 1.3). Turn right, cross 8th Street, bear right into the parking lot and pick up Kestrel Trail #39A, heading east to Crestline. It's a gradual climb up the gulch, and then turn left at the top of the hill on Crestline Trail #28 (mile 2.4). Follow Crestline 1.2 miles to the junction with Sidewinder (mile 3.6). Turn right and ride Sidewinder to the Trail #4 junction (mile 5). Take a breather, and then descend on Trail #4 to the Crestline Trail (mile 5.6). Then -- now here comes the bruiser part -- turn around and ride back up Trail #4. Ouch. Back at the Sidewinder saddle (mile 6.2), turn right and ride Sidewinder back to Crestline (mile 7.6). Turn right on Crestline and ride to the Hulls-Crestline junction and ride up to the motorcycle parking lot on 8th Street (mile 9.1). Cross 8th Street, and ride Trail #1 to the Bob's Trail junction (mile 9.9). Turn left and ride Bob's to the bottom (mile 11.6). Turn left on the paved road and follow it to Braemere, turn right and follow Braemere across Curling, down to 15th Street. Turn left at 15th and Hill, and follow 13th to Lucky 13 in Hyde Park (mile 14.5). Time for pizza and beer!

Jenny says the Bomb Squad typically breaks into two groups -- one group that rides hard in preparation for an upcoming race, and another group that might enjoy a more low-key social ride. The group is open to women only during the week; co-ed outings on weekends. Guys can ride with the Bomb Squad during the week, but they have to wear a skirt. So far, no takers. If you want more information on the Bomb Squad, email Jenny at bombb-owner@yahoogroups.com or call 371-9202.

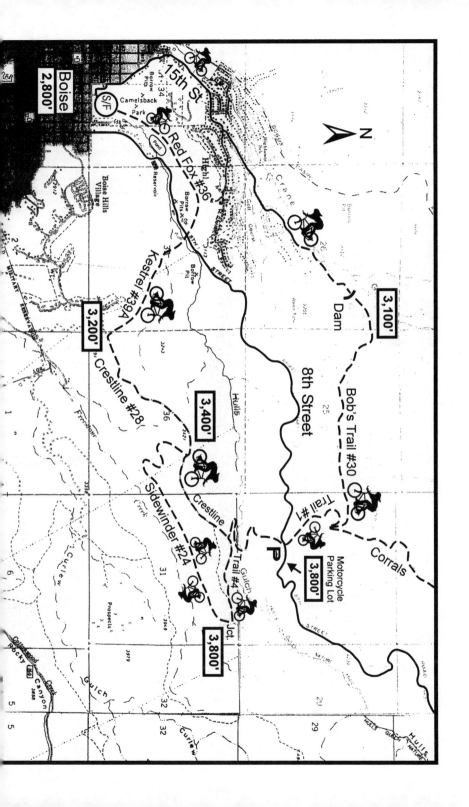

CHRIS' FAVORITE LUNCH RIDE

Quality: ****
Distance: 9.1 miles
Difficulty: Advanced
Riding time: 1-1.5 hours
Trail: Nearly all singletrack
Season: Spring to fall
Watch out for: Joggers, walkers, dogs, etc.

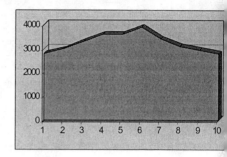

Chris Haunold

Getting there: Ride or drive to the end of north 9th Street, or the east end of Camel's Back Park. The ride starts here.

The Ride: This is my "lunch ride," when I have about an hour of free time, and I want to get maximum time on dirt. The other cool part about this ride is that you ride almost completely on singletrack for almost 10 miles, and it features two significant climbs – up Hulls Gulch, and then up Trail #4, a trail I call "the Stairway to Hell." If needed, I can cut off part of the ride if I am dragging or I don't have much time.

To begin, I leave the shop and noodle my way through the North End, taking any number of streets to the end of 9th Street, next to the east side of Camel's Back Park. Head up the dirt trail, take a right on Hulls Pond Loop, and then head north on the two-track to a parking area and 8th Street. Cross 8th Street directly and pick up Owl's Roost, a singletrack, and ride on a slight uphill grade to Kestrel Trail #39A (mile 1.1 from 9th Street Trailhead). Take a sharp left and ride to the Lower Hulls parking area and pick up the Lower Hulls Gulch Trail #29 on the north end of the parking lot. Ride up Hulls and turn left and cross the bridge at the junction with the bottom of Red Cliffs Trail. It's about two miles of climbing to the Hulls Gulch-Crestline junction (mile 3.6). Turn right, cross over the creek and ride the Freeway Trail (Crestline) about ¼ mile to the bottom of Trail #4, the "Stairway to Hell," as I like to call it. Take a sharp left and climb the steep trail to Sidewinder saddle (mile 4.4). Take a breather. You'll need it. Hang a right and cruise down Sidewinder back to the Freeway (mile 5.8). Turn left on the Freeway and ride to the Red Cliffs Trail junction (mile 6.3), and enjoy the fast descent down to the sand pit at the bottom. Veer to the left and ride back to the Lower Hulls parking lot. Cross 8th Street, and ride Red Fox past the water tank back to the 9th Street Trailhead (mile 9.1). I usually cut through Camel's Back Park and then just blast down 10th street back to the shop. The ride is 12 miles round trip from Idaho Mountain Touring. It can be shortened if you don't have enough time or you're tired. I like this ride because it has maximum dirt time with lots of climbing and good descending. -- Chris H.

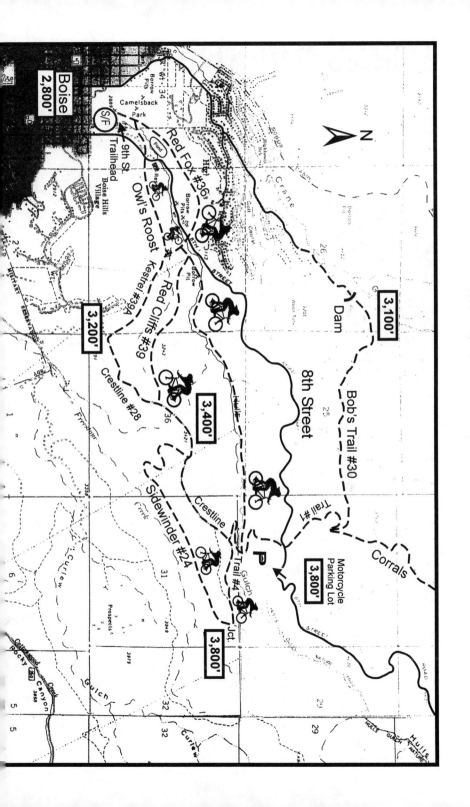

STUEBIE'S DEATH MARCH

Quality: ****
Distance: 21.5 miles
Difficulty: Advanced
Riding time: 2.5-3 hours
Trail: Singletrack, two-track
Season: Spring to fall
Watch out for: Other trail users

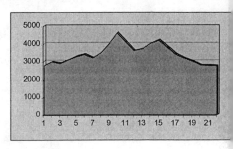

Steve Stuebner

Getting there:
Ride or drive
to Fort Boise
Park, by the intersection of Mountain Cove Road and
Reserve Street. The ride starts here.

The Ride: If I've got a couple hours of free time, and I'm
itching for a good workout, this is one of my favorite routes
in the foothills. Some of my friends call it the Stuebner
"death march." It involves a fairly brutal climb up Trail #5
ridge to Trail #4, and then a tricky downhill involving sand,
ruts and death cookies on Trail #4 to Crestline, and then
climbing over 8th Street to ride Corrals backwards, and then
out on Bob's Trail. **To begin**, ride out of the Fort Boise

parking lot to Reserve Street, turn left and ride up Reserve to Shaw Mountain Road
and climb to the junction with Table Rock Road (mile 1.5). Bear left on Rocky
Canyon Road. Follow it to the end of the pavement (mile 2.7) and ride to Shane's
Trailhead (mile 3.3). Take Shane's up the hill, riding on singletrack now. Bear left
at the Y-junction at the first saddle, and ride to the junction with Trail #26 and
#26A (mile 5.2). Go left on #26, descend into a creek bottom, cross the creek, and
get into first gear for an abrupt steep climb at mile 5.5. Follow the trail as it joins a
two-track, going downhill, to the Trail #5 trailhead at mile 6.1. Turn right and
crank up the sandy singletrack as it climbs the ridge. Conserve energy for a couple
of bad-ass climbs coming up. At mile 7, get into your granny gears and climb a
nasty, increasingly sandy hill. Try to select the cleanest line and you might make it.
Keep climbing. At mile 8.2, ignore the junction on the right with Trail #6. Go
straight and climb less than a mile to the Trail #4 junction (mile 8.9). Take a
breather, turn left and cruise down Trail #4 to Sidewinder junction (mile 10.2). It's
steep and sandy with lots of ruts. At Sidewinder junction, bear right and descend
Trail #4 to Crestline. Turn right, and climb to the motorcycle parking lot (mile
11.4). Ride across 8th Street and take Trail #1, a singletrack, west and ride Corrals
backwards, arriving at the summit at mile 13.8. Now, you're ready to enjoy a rapid
descent back to the Bob's Junction (mile 15.4). Turn right on Bob's and rock on
down the trail to the paved cul de sac (mile 17.2). Turn left and follow the paved
road to Braemere Road, turn right and cruise downhill to Curling Drive. Cross
Curling and ride 15th Street back to Boise, turn left on Fort, and return to Fort Boise
(mile 21.2). You've earned your dinner.

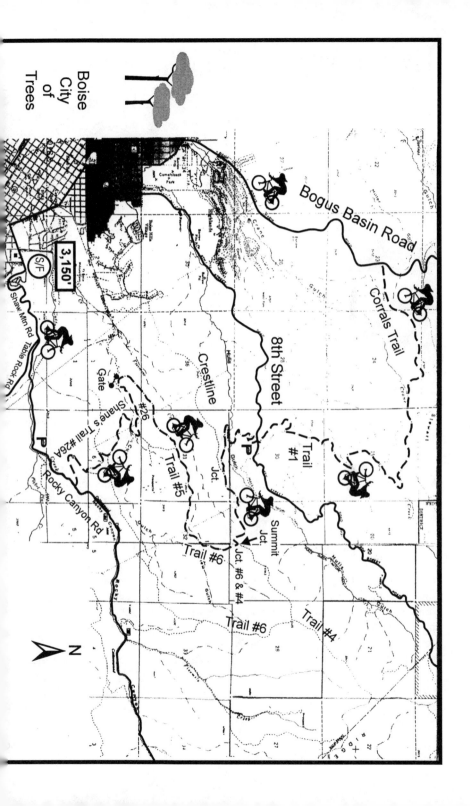

Boise
City
of
Trees

N

TOM'S FAVORITE SINGLETRACK

Quality: ***
Distance: 14 miles
Difficulty: Advanced
Riding time: 1:45 to 2 hours
Trail: Two-track, single-track
Season: April-October
Special note: Please observe winter closure for wintering deer.
Getting there: Head east on the Greenbelt, past Eckert Road, to Council Springs Road. Turn left and ride straight for the foothills to a Fish and Game gate (5 miles from Municipal Park). The ride starts here.

Tom Platt

The Ride: This is one of Tom Platt's favorite rides in the Foothills. He calls it the Trough Loop after a number of cattle troughs that you ride by on the way down the mountain. "The ride has a lot of good climbing in it, some fun descents and true singletrack, somewhat of a rare thing in the Foothills," he says. For folks who live in Southeast Boise, this loop is a real keeper local ride. For the rest of us, it's a sweet alternative that must be visited frequently.

To begin the ride, hoist your bike over the gate and proceed up the two-track road. After climbing for .4 miles, shift into low gear for the first of many major steeps in this route. Go right at a junction at .7 miles. Keep climbing. After the fifth hill, you'll arrive at a saddle junction for Trail #8 at mile 2.1. Go right on Trail #12 and cruise over some rolling terrain and a series of whoop-dee-doos. Then, you're climbing again. At mile 3.6, pass by junction with Trail #13. Continue climbing on Trail #12 to the junction with Trail E (mile 4.9). Go left and climb several steep pitches to the upper junction with Trail #9 (mile 6.5). Go right on the primitive two-track and enjoy a fast descent back to Trail E and a wooden gate (mile 7.7). Go through the gate, and close it behind you. Veer off to the right and pick up Tom's favorite foothills singletrack, a sweet narrow thing, as it winds down the grassy slopes of the Boise River Wildlife Management Area. Tom has seen several deer herds here in the spring. Follow the singletrack on the brisk downhill, past the cattle troughs (mile 8.3). Stay with the trail when it crosses Highland Valley Road (mile 8.9). Now you're descending on Trail #11 to the trailhead (mile 11.4). Follow the paved road down the hill to Warm Springs Avenue and the Crow Inn. Pick up the Greenbelt behind the Crow Inn and ride back to the Squaw Creek Trailhead (mile 14) or wherever you live.

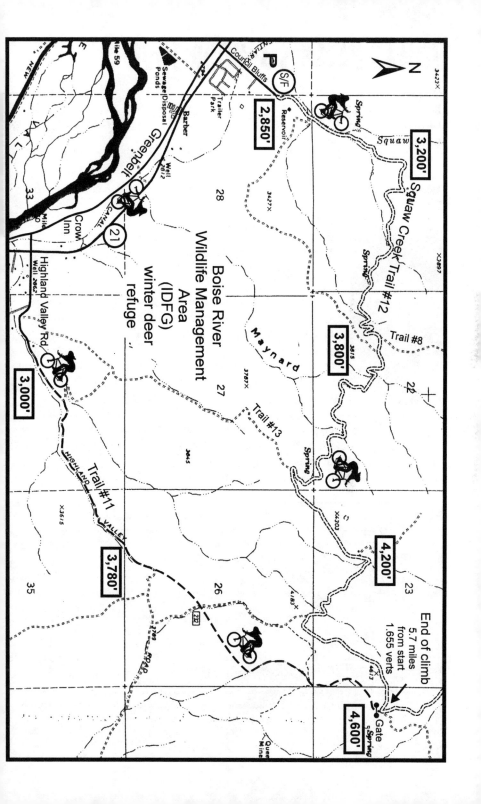

TOMAS PATEK'S 3-HOUR TOUR

Quality: ****
Distance: 26.8 miles
Difficulty: Expert
Riding time: 3.5-5 hours
Trail: Singletrack, two-track
Season: June-early October
Watch out for: ATVs and vehicles on Boise Ridge Road; hidden corners on the Dry Creek Trail.

Tomas Patek

Getting there: Ride or drive to the lower Hulls Gulch Trailhead, off of north 8th Street, after it turns to dirt at the base of the foothills, on the right-hand side of the road. The ride starts here.

The Ride: This is Tomas Patek's favorite ride in the foothills. Tomas and his wife Therese, own World Cycle, on 8th Street in downtown Boise. Tomas says he rode this in 3.5 hours ... if you can do that, I say you're a foothills master-blaster. Tom has experienced cougar *growls* in Dry Creek, so pay attention. **To begin,** head up Hulls Gulch Trail #29 to the Motorcycle Parking lot. "I love to start the majority of my longer rides climbing up Hulls Gulch. The moderately technical singletrack climb along the creek sure beats the dusty route up 8th Street."

Mile 2.7 Cross 8th Street, pick up Trail #1 across the dirt road, and ride up Corrals backwards. "Watch out for two challenging corners. If you ride this trail in this direction as fast as you can, you know what I'm talking about. The

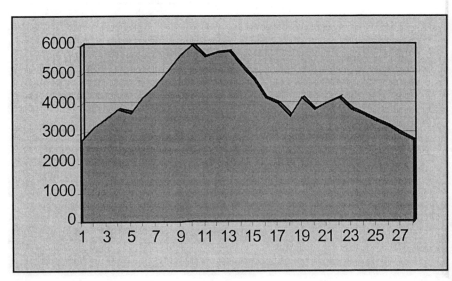

112

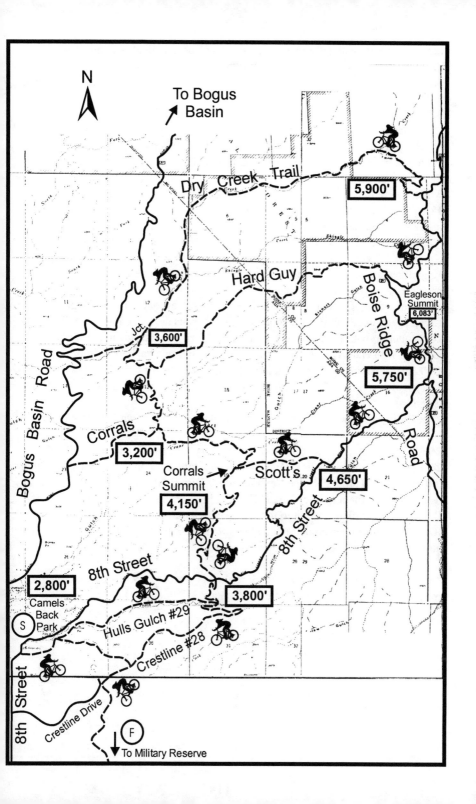

left-hand corner just before the intersection of Bob's Trail always puts a smile on my face. Settle down and get ready to climb."

5.2 Corrals Summit. Veer to the right on Scott's Trail and ride the steep singletrack to 8th Street.

6.2 Reach Scott's junction with 8th Street. Turn left and climb 8th Street to the Boise Ridge Road. Lots of steep climbing on a scratchy gravel and rocky jeep trail.

8.2 Ridge Road junction. You've just climbed 3,000 verts from the valley floor. Turn left and ride over Eagleson Summit to the Upper Dry Creek junction. "The pine scent of the forest and the cooler temperatures make all the climbing worthwhile. There have been cougars seen on this section of the ride so pay attention."

12 Upper Dry Creek junction. Peel off on the singletrack on the left and follow it into a steep descent into the densely timbered watershed, and then many creek crossings. See Page 80 for the Dry Creek description. "The view from the top of Upper Dry Creek is fantastic. I always stop at the beginning section of this singletrack and admire the bit of exposure on this ridge. The descent into Dry Creek is challenging but fun, especially with a few good friends. This is the spot where at dusk I heard my first cougar growl. This made the rest of the ride through Dry Creek pretty exciting. Be sure to look for paw prints near standing water."

16.8 Junction with Hard Guy connector trail. Turn left and ride to the saddle junction with Hard Guy. Go straight, downhill, and ride back to Corrals.

18.7 Junction with Corrals. Turn left and ride to the top of Corrals, and then over to 8th Street via Trail #1. Cross 8th Street and descend to the Hulls Gulch-Crestline junction.

22.8 Hulls-Crestline junction. Cross the creek and cruise down Crestline to the trailhead.

25.5 Junction of Crestline trailhead and Military Reserve Connector Trail #23.

26.4 After dropping down to Military Reserve, turn right on the dirt road, and then left and climb Trail #22 to the Central Ridge. Turn right at the top of the ridge, and descend to the main trailhead area. Then, ride across to pick up the bottom of the Black Forest Trail and ride it to the end, where it dumps out on a concrete apron. Ride your bike to the singletrack on the left and exit the trail by the dog-play area along Mountain Cove Road. End mileage: 26.8.

"Finishing up the ride via the route described is just my way of trying to ride the most singletrack on my way home for dinner." - Tomas Patek.

BACK OF BEYOND 8-HOUR TOUR

Quality: ****
Distance: 50 miles
Difficulty: Expert
Riding time: 7-9 hours
Trail: Dirt road, two-track, singletrack, paved road
Season: July-October
Watch out for: Motorcycles, ATVs, vehicles, bears, loggers, equestrians

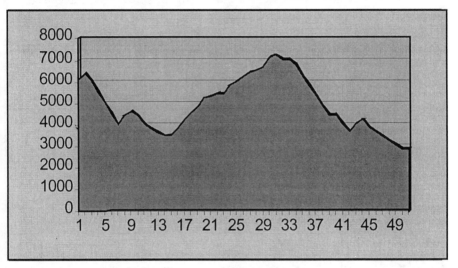

Here is the very definition of an ass-kicking ride.

Getting there: We recommend that you have a friend drop you off at Eagleson Summit to start this ride. If you prefer, ride up 8th Street however you like to the junction with the Boise Ridge Road (8.5 miles and 3,000-foot vertical rise from Boise). Turn left onto the Ridge Road and ride to the summit (about 1 mile from the 8th Street-Ridge Road junction).

The Ride: The beauty of this ride is that it starts in the Boise Front, but it takes you over the ridge into Boise County to experience some incredible scenery and new terrain. Based on the mileage, and multiple climbs involved, this should be considered an endurance ride. It should be attempted only by those who have the ability to climb steep trails and endure rough descents for hours at a time. Be sure to carry plenty of food and water. Three of us, Chris Hahn, Rene Mullen and Lisa King, rode this route on a hot day in July. Afterwards, we all agreed that a cool, crisp autumn day would be best for this ride, since the heat made the climbing that much tougher! But it's well worth the trip to see some spectacular new scenery and get to know the "back side" of the ridge.

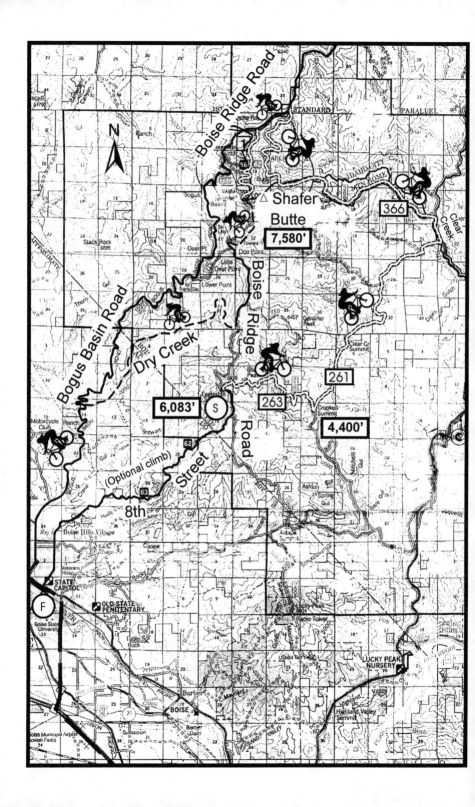

To begin: At Eagleson Summit, turn right from the Boise Ridge Road onto U.S. Forest Service Road #263. Follow signs indicating "Crooked Summit - 5 miles."

Mile 0.6 Bear right at "Y".

1.3 Bear right, continuing on the jeep road. Here begins a nice long descent.

5.1 Reach bottom of jeep road, which dumps into Clear Creek Road, a well-developed dirt road (there is no road sign). Take a left to descend and then climb towards Clear Creek Summit.

7.6 Clear Creek Summit – signed with a "No Winter Maintenance" sign. Begin rolling descent toward the town of Clear Creek.

11.5 Arrive in Clear Creek on pavement. On the left, there is a restaurant/ bar, now

Rene Mullen, Chris Hahn and Lisa King

closed. If it reopens sometime, it'd be your last chance to buy food and drink. Continue on the road until it T's into Grimes Creek Road.

12.8 Reach T intersection at Grimes Creek Road. Turn left. Keep an eye out for the turnoff to Pine Creek Road on the left, less than a mile away.

13.6 Junction with Pine Creek Rd, Forest Road #366. Take a left. This is a privately maintained road. Small spurs, trails, and tracks go off on either side, but ignore them; stay on the main road. The road follows Pine Creek for a while, then it leaves the creek.

18.2 A dirt road (currently with "road closed" sign) Y's off to the left, heading straight toward Shafer Butte. Ignore this and stay on main road going right. Immediately after this junction, the climb begins to level off and becomes a rim road with spectacular views of the valley below -- a great place to stop for lunch.

22.5 The road opens into a large clearing and the ridge, which has been on your left, dips to meet the road. The main road hairpins left; follow this, curving sharply.

25.1 Pine Creek Road T-s into Boise Ridge Road (signed as Forest Road #374).

Take a left on the Boise Ridge Road, continuing to climb.

26.4 A singletrack, the Mores Mountain Trail, heads off the left side of road, signed as "Trail 190." Turn left and ride the whoop-dee-dos uphill. Beautiful views are visible on the left. Follow "190" sign when trail splits.

28 Arrive at Shafer Butte Campground. Here, there are latrines and a faucet to refill water bottles, both open during the summer season. You will see the top of Shafer Butte looming above you. Leaving the campground area, go right on the dirt road, pass the campground fee payment kiosk, then take an immediate left on the paved road toward the "Group camping" area, passing around the gate. Keep an eye out for a dirt trail that goes off to the right from the parking lot in about 50 yards. Take this trail, going around a second gate, and begin the switchback climb up to Shafer Butte. Look for a large ski area sign that says "Paradise Access." Follow the sign down a doubletrack, watching for an unsigned singletrack which veers off to the right after a few yards. Follow the singletrack, which becomes a rough doubletrack in about a mile. When this trail splits, follow the track to the left for a short descent. Continue to follow the trail crossing a wide grassy slope, the "Nugget" run in the ski season. Cross this run and continue on the trail, which climbs for a short while then descends rather steeply.

31 The singletrack joins a dirt road. Follow this toward the radio towers ahead.

31.7 Radio towers summit at the top of Deer Point. Stop underneath the shady tree. Here begins the initial descent on the Boise Ridge.

31.9 The road splits. Decision point!! If anyone in your group is not up for a technical descent or is having mechanical problems, this is a great opportunity for a quick descent to the right; this limb of the Ridge Road will take you down to Bogus Basin Road for a smooth descent on pavement. If you are still feeling fresh, bear left on Ridge Road, and follow us down Dry Creek.

35.4 Junction on the right. A singletrack dips initially downward, then climbs slightly and curves right, going around a ridge. This is the entry to Dry Creek. Follow the trail, ever downward, into Dry Creek, bearing right at 35.6 miles where the trail splits. Descend!! Look forward to multiple creek crossings and abrupt, steep climbs. The Dry Creek trail is described in detail elsewhere in this book.

On our way out, we rode the Dry Creek connector to Hard Guy and Corrals, climbed over the Corrals Summit, and then cruised back home down Hulls Gulch. What a ride! Congratulations on completing a really tough loop! -- Chris Hahn

RIDE TO MARK'S CABIN

Quality: ****
Distance: 55 miles
Difficulty: Expert
Riding time: 8 hours
Trail: Paved road, dirt road, two-track, singletrack
Season: June-October
Watch out for: Vehicles, horseback riders

Mark Anderson

Getting there: Ride or drive to Camel's Back Park, at the junction of 13th Street and Heron Street in Boise's North End. The ride starts here.

The Ride: This is one major whopper of a ride for those who have the endurance to pedal all day and tackle multiple climbs. Mark Anderson pioneered this route because it drops out in Garden Valley right next to his cabin. I rode it with him and four other guys in the October rain in 2001. We still loved the whole experience of covering so much countryside. You can shorten the route considerably by starting from Bogus Basin, thereby avoiding the arduous 16-mile, 3,500-vertical-foot climb to the ski area. Be sure to pack lots of water and food.

To begin, head out of Camel's Back Park and follow 13th Street north around to Bogus Basin Road. Turn right and spin up the paved road. Conserve as much as energy as possible on the relentless climb.

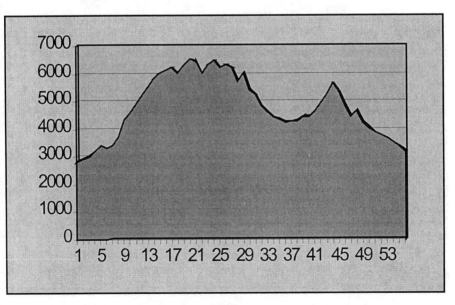

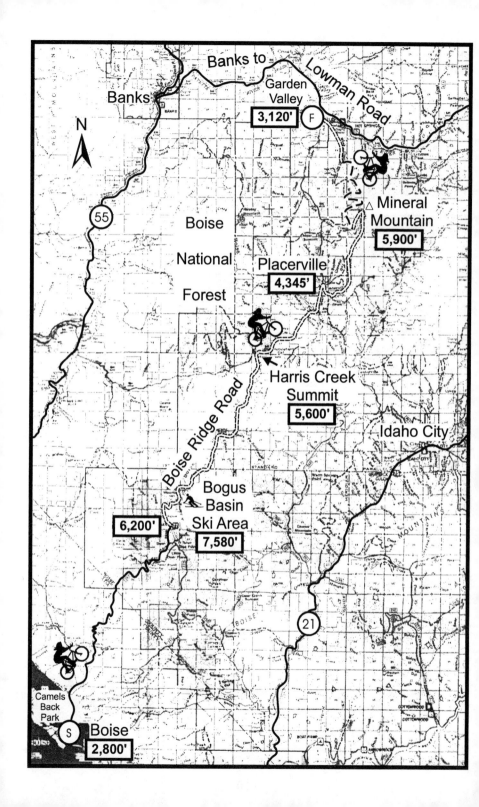

16.5 Bogus Creek Lodge. Bear left and follow the Boise Ridge Road for the next 14 miles. It's a narrow primitive dirt road that will take you up and down along the Boise Ridge like a yo-yo. Conserve energy!

19.6 Turnoff to Mores Mountain picnic area. The ridge road gets markedly more narrow. Ignore many sideroads for the next 12 miles.

30.2 Encounter major five-way junction at Harris Creek Summit. Turn right on USFS Road #615, and enjoy a fast descent on a wide dirt road to the Placerville-Centerville junction.

34.8 Reach the junction, marked by a red shelter for a group of mailboxes. Turn right on USFS Road #307 and follow it to a signed left-hand turn for the Ophir Creek Road.

35.4 Turn left on Ophir Creek Road. Climb gradually along a nifty meadow for the next 8 miles.

37.1 Go left and then an immediate right by a ponderosa pine.

37.4 Bear right on USFS Road #386. Ignore side junctions for the next couple miles.

39.8 Road forks, bear left on USFS Road #386C. Climbing at a steeper pitch now.

40 Turn right at fork.

42 Go left at two-way junction and continue climbing.

42.8 Come to T-junction with USFS Road #395 at top of hill. Go right.

43.1 Go left at junction with USFS Road #648. Going down!

43.7 Go right at two-way junction.

45.2 Go left at two-way junction and ride on park-like two-track.

45.8 Junction on right. Go right.

45.9 Merge with road. Bear right.

46.5 Junction on left. Go straight and climb for a short distance and then zoom downhill some more.

49.7 Come to abrupt hill for 2/10ths of a mile. And then ride downhill again.

50.8 Junction on left with primitive two-track. Bear right and stay on main road.

51.7 Go left on Wash Creek Road and cruise downhill.

53.5 Junction of Wash Creek Road and South Fork Payette River Road. Go left and ride on the South Fork Road to the Alder Creek Bridge parking area. Mark's Cabin is nearly straight across the road, down to the right. Wouldn't it be nice if you had a cabin on the South Fork at this moment in time?

55 Reach the Alder Creek Road-South Fork Road junction, turn right and you'll ride up to your vehicle at the parking area. You made it!

Winter/Spring Training Rides

Once it starts to rain in the late fall or early November, the trail-riding season is over in the Boise Foothills. Please do not ride on singletrack trails during the late fall and winter months. At this time of year, the trails are highly vulnerable to erosion due to freezing and thawing temperatures, and typically heavy precipitation — either in the form of rain or snow. Anyone who violates this basic backcountry code should be sentenced to a year of hard labor repairing trails with deep tire divots and gouges.

Fortunately, there are a number of well-compacted dirt roads and nifty "roadie" pavement loops that cyclists can ride in the off season to stay in shape. Here is a list of my favorites, including mileage, and approximate riding time. Be sure to use your best judgment when attempting any of the dirt roads listed below.

Foothills East Training Loop

Distance: 2.3 miles
Time: 10-20 minutes per loop
Watch out for: Cars backing out of driveways; children playing on sidewalks and in the street.
The Ride: This is a great combo training ride — short hills and fast descents through Boise's East End and Foothills East. I discovered this loop while watching professional road racers whiz by my front yard on East Washington in 1986. **To begin,** ride to Reserve Street (adjacent to Fort Boise) and head for the mountains. Near the bottom of the foothills, you'll pass Avenue H on the right. The mileage starts here. Proceed on Reserve to Shaw Mountain Road; turn right and ride up the medium grade for .9 miles. This hill is almost continuous with a new view around each corner. It's three separate pulls to the top. Turn right on Shenandoah, climb the little steep pitch and then zoom down the hill for .7 miles, being ready to stop at a moment's notice for children or cars. Follow the downhill plunge to the bottom of the hill (past Pierce) and turn left on Locust. This is a through street to East Washington. Turn right and push it hard on the flat toward the T-junction. This is a through street as well. At the stop sign, turn left and then take an immediate right on Avenue H. Pound some more on the flat. It's a half mile to Reserve Street. Turn right, and head up Shaw Mountain for another loop. Try to do three or four loops in an hour. **Variations:** Reverse the loop. It's a much steeper climb up Shenandoah, but it's shorter than Shaw Mountain. Mix it up.

HILL ROAD-GREENBELT LOOP

Distance: 11-plus miles
Time: 1-3 hours
Watch out for: Cars and goat heads on Hill Road. Yield to pedestrians and dial down your speed on the Greenbelt.
The Ride: Barring major snow and ice, this ride can be done year-round. **To begin,** ride to the intersection of Bogus Basin Road and Hill Road in the North End of Boise. Mileage starts here. Proceed west on Hill Road. It's 4.5 miles to Gary Lane. You'll pass 36th Street at 1.6 miles, Collister at 2.5 miles. Turn right at 2.8 miles and follow Hill as it jogs to the north and then west again. Pierce Park peels off at mile 4.0. Keep going another .6 miles to the stop light at Gary Lane. Turn left. Enjoy the wide, striped bike lane. It's a little over a mile to State Street. Proceed across the intersection on Glenwood. Be wary of cars; this is a very busy intersection. Ride south on Glenwood to the bridge crossing the Boise River. Jump up on the sidewalk, cross the river, and then drop into the underpass for the Greenbelt. Head east on the Greenbelt along the Fairgrounds and Les Bois Park. It's five miles to Julia Davis Park, where you can drop off the path on Broadway. The total loop is about 11 miles, depending on where you live and where you peel off from the Greenbelt.

CARTWRIGHT-PIERCE PARK-HILL ROAD LOOP

Distance: 10.6 miles
Time: 1.5-3 hours
Watch out for: Cars, target shooters and goat heads.
The Ride: This is one of the best off-season rides because it features some hill-climbing, pleasant scenery and fun descents. **To begin,** ride to the intersection of Hill Road and Bogus Basin Road in Boise's North End. Mileage starts here. Ride north on Bogus Basin Road, scale the first hill, and then watch for a left-hand turn on Cartwright Road after the Mormon Church and before J.R. Simplot's house on the green hill. Turn left on Cartwright. The road rises quickly for .7 miles to an initial summit. Once over the top, you'll cruise downhill on pavement by the Cartwright Ranch and airstrip. Then, the road climbs again for 1.4 miles to a second, higher summit (mile 3.6). Now it's a half-mile to the Pierce Park turnoff on the left. This is a well-marked junction as Cartwright Road continues on to the right toward Lower Dry Creek. Turn left to ride down Pierce Park, a narrow dirt road that parallels a lush draw called Pierce Gulch. It's 2.6 miles to Hill Road, nearly all downhill (mile 6.6). Turn left at Hill to complete the loop to Bogus Basin Road. It's about 4 miles to the start. Total mileage: 10.6.

CARTWRIGHT-DRY CREEK-SEAMAN'S GULCH LOOP

Distance: 16.6 miles
Time: 2-4 hours
Watch out for: Cars, target shooters, goat heads, livestock.
The Ride: This is the best and longest rolling-hills training ride in the valley that's rideable practically year-round. It's very similar to the Pierce Park loop except it's longer, and has two additional hills. To start, ride to the intersection of Hill Road and Bogus Basin Road in Boise's North End. Mileage starts here. Scale the first hill on Bogus and then turn left on Cartwright Road (.8 miles). The road rises quickly for .7 miles to an initial summit. Cruise down the pavement by the Cartwright Ranch and airstrip. Then, the road climbs again for 1.4 miles to a second, higher summit (mile 3.6). Now it's a half-mile to the Pierce Park turnoff on the left. This is a well-marked junction (mile 4.1) as Cartwright Road continues to the right toward Lower Dry Creek. Turn right on Cartwright, climb a quick hill to a third summit and enjoy a one-mile downhill to the Lower Dry Creek Valley. At mile 5.5, you'll come to a junction of Dry Creek Road and Cartwright Road. Go left, leave the pavement and ride along the valley. (Cartwright Road dead-ends at private property). At mile 7.2, turn left and cross the creek. It's about a mile to the Seaman's Gulch junction. At that point, bear left and take the paved road back to Hill Road. You'll climb for 1.4 miles to the top (mile 9.6). Now, it's all downhill for two miles to Hill Road (mile 11.6). Turn left. It's five miles back to the Bogus Basin junction.

GREENBELT-AMITY-GOWEN-KOOTENAI LOOP

Distance: 18.5 miles
Time: 1-2.5 hours
Watch out for: Cars, low-flying planes.
The Ride: To roadies, this is a well-known loop ride on mostly flat terrain. The ride is long enough, and runs in several different directions such that you're sure to pick up a headwind or two, which will enhance the workout. Of course, it's huge fun to get behind a tailwind on this ride, too. **To begin,** ride the Greenbelt to Walnut near Municipal Park and the M-K Nature Center. Mileage starts here. Ride in an easterly direction, through the Warm Springs Golf Course, to Eckert Road (mile 4.2). Turn right and follow the Greenbelt path to the junction of Barber Park, Eckert Road and Boise Avenue. Go straight on Eckert and follow it as it turns into Amity Road around the corner. It's exactly two miles to a stop sign at Federal Way (mile 5.2). Amity has a very thin shoulder. As you're heading west on Amity, note the left-hand turn to the Oregon Trail subdivision. At Federal Way, turn left and head for Gowen Road (mile 5.8). Turn right at the stop light, cross under the freeway and take a tour around the southern fringe of the airport. Gowen starts out with virtually no shoulder, but within a mile, it turns into a nice three-foot bike lane. It's 5.5 miles from the Gowen/I-84 intersection to the point where Gowen takes a big bend to the north and joins Orchard Street at the junction with I-84 (mile 13.7). Stay with Orchard and drop into the busy intersection of Orchard and Overland (mile 14.7).

Wait for the green light and proceed to Kootenai Street (mile 15) just past the shopping center. Turn right. Now it's a straight cruise across the Boise Bench area for two miles on a street with a bike lane. Cross Vista at mile 16.3 and proceed to the junction of Protest and Federal Way (mile 16.7). Turn left on Protest, descend the hill, cross Boise Avenue and head toward Broadway on Beacon. One block before Broadway, turn left on Dakota Street (17.5) to avoid the Beacon-Broadway intersection. Go several blocks to University Drive. Turn right and head for the Broadway-University traffic light. Turn left on Broadway and proceed just past the Boise River bridge, then duck into the Greenbelt on a short hill just past the bridge (mile 18). Now it's less than a half-mile back to the Walnut intersection (mile 18.4). You made it!

GREENBELT-ECKERT ROAD-GREENBELT LOOP

Distance: 10 miles
Time: 45 minutes-2 hours
Watch out for: Cars, people on the Greenbelt
The Ride: Start at the intersection of Walnut Street and the Greenbelt next to Municipal Park in east Boise. Mileage starts here. Ride in an easterly direction, through the Warm Springs Golf Course, to Eckert Road (mile 4.3). Turn right on the new bike path and proceed across the Boise River to Barber Park (mile 4.9). Pick up the Greenbelt on the south side of the river next to the entrance booth and ride west on the Greenbelt. The path winds through the park, and then bear left into a small park in a half-mile. The pathway winds through several developments for a mile or so until it ducks into the woods for a short period and then dumps out on ParkCenter Boulevard. (Be sure to stay on the bike path, and stay off the walking path next to the river.) Follow the paved bike path on the shoulder of ParkCenter to River Run Drive (mile 7.3) and turn right. Follow the bike lane on the shoulder of the road to the Cottonwood condos (mile 8.3). Watch for the link to the Greenbelt path at the entrance to the condos. Cruise behind the business complex in ParkCenter, turn right on the new walk bridge across the Boise River, and then follow the Greenbelt back to Municipal Park.

GREENBELT-HIGHLAND VALLEY SUMMIT & BACK

Distance: 26 miles (roundtrip)
Time: 2-3.5 hours
Watch out for: Cars, folks on the Greenbelt
The Ride: This is a good out-and-back training ride because of the sustained 4.5-mile climb from Discovery Park to Highland Valley Summit. It's also a ride that cyclists can do under just about any weather conditions, except for deep snow and ice. To begin, ride to the intersection of Walnut Street and the Greenbelt next to Municipal Park in east Boise. Mileage starts here. Ride east on the Greenbelt for 8.6 miles to Discovery Park. Follow the path through the park and then jump onto Idaho 21 for the steady uphill climb to Highland Valley Summit. It's 4.5 miles to

the top. The first mile up to the top of Lucky Peak Dam is steeper than the next section, which flattens out a bit until the road bends to the right, and it's a fairly steep grade to the final pull to the summit (mile 13). Stop at the Hilltop Cafe for a hot drink and snack. Then zoom back to Discovery Park, pick up the Greenbelt and enjoy the ride back to Boise (mile 26).

ROCKY CANYON-ROBIE CREEK-GREENBELT LOOP

Distance: 37.5 miles
Time: 3.5-5 hours
Watch out for: Cars, folks on the Greenbelt
The Ride: This is the longest and toughest off-season ride in the book. It's best to try this ride in late April or May, when the snowpack is melted off Aldape Summit. Otherwise, you'll have to hike through snow and ice to get over the top. To begin, ride up Rocky Canyon Road 6.5 miles to Aldape Summit. Once on top, it's a six-mile plunge into Robie Creek, where the pavement begins again. Follow the main road about three miles to Idaho 21 (mile 15.5). Turn right. It's 22 miles back to Boise. Climb the first grade and enjoy a slight downhill cruise back to the Mores Creek Bridge (mile 22). From here, it's a long gradual climb to Highland Valley Summit (mile 24.5). Take a break at the Hilltop Cafe. Now it's 13 miles back to Boise, all downhill. Of course, you could face a headwind on the flat grind back along the Greenbelt to Boise (mile 37.5).

BOISE RIVER GREENBELT-LOWER OREGON TRAIL

This route is about 20 miles long and takes 1.5 to 3.5 hours, depending on your route, riding skill and endurance. See pages 46 and 66 for possible variations on combining a ride on the Oregon Trail with the Geenbelt to form a loop. In the off-season, it's best to try the Oregon Trail portion of this loop when the two-track road is frozen hard. Anything in between will be quite muddy.

8TH STREET

It's about 8 miles to the top of 8th Street, but in the off-season, you won't be able to ride to the top once the snowpack sets in. So your trip will be probably limited to riding 5-6 miles up the ridge. This may take 1.5-2.5 hours, depending on ability. In a typical winter, it's difficult to reach Scott's Trail on 8th Street until the snow and ice begin to melt in late February or early March. This road is fairly well graveled and sandy, so it absorbs a large amount of moisture before it turns into "gumbo." **To begin,** ride or drive to the Foothills parking area on north 8th Street, about a half-mile from the end of the pavement. It's 3.2 miles to the BLM gate, and 3.5 miles to the motorcycle parking lot. When the road is clear, you can ride 8.5

miles to the 8th Street-Ridge Road junction. Ride as far as you can, depending on riding conditions, snow and ice, the mud factor, and your endurance.

ROCKY CANYON ROAD

In the winter, the last mile or two of Rocky Canyon Road gets snowbound about two miles from Aldape Summit (elevation 4,800 feet). In a drought winter, it can be possible to ride nearly to the top. This road is extremely sandy and well graveled, so it is rideable most of the time in the lower reaches. **To start,** ride or drive from Fort Boise (Reserve Street and Fort Street junction) north on Reserve Street to Shaw Mountain Road, bear right and follow Shaw Mountain to the junction with Table Rock Road at the top of Foothills East. Bear left and follow Rocky Canyon Road about 1 mile to the end of the pavement. Cruise up Rocky Canyon Road, as far as ice, snow, mud allow, 6.5 miles to Aldape Summit. It's an 1,800 vertical foot climb. In typical years, the snow line begins between Five-Mile Creek and Orchard Gulch, blocking riders from reaching the last mile or so to the summit. At times, the snow and ice can get compacted to a rideable consistency, for the especially skilled rider, and of course, those with snow tires.

TABLE ROCK ROAD

This road is rideable nearly year-round, except after extremely heavy rainstorms or heavy snow at low elevations in December or January. The road is paved now from Table Rock Road to a point where it is a quarter-mile from the summit. See page 64 for descriptions on riding to Table Rock. For the winter ride, ride up Table Road Road to the top, and avoid the dirt trails. The clay soil in this area gives a new meaning to "gumbo."

SWAN FALLS LOOP

Several cool loops can be found in the Snake River Birds of Prey Natural Conservation Area, beginning at Swan Falls Dam. These trails often can be ridden throughout the winter. See "Mountain Biking Idaho" for details on that ride and several others in Owyhee County, not to mention a total of 80 rides statewide.

FYI-KEY CONTACTS

MOUNTAIN BIKERS' RESOURCE GUIDE :
(All phone numbers 208 area code)

TRAIL CONDITIONS, CAMPING INFORMATION:
Boise Front trails hotline: 384-4044
Ridge to Rivers trail coordinator: 384-3360
Bureau of Land Management, Boise field office: 384-3300
Boise Parks System (Greenbelt): 384-4240
Ada County Parks & Waterways: 343-1328
Boise National Forest: 373-4100
Bogus Basin Ski Area: 332-5100
Idaho Parks & Recreation Dept. trail coordinator: 334-4180 ext. 228

TRAIL GROUPS:
Consider helping these groups work on trail-improvement projects:
❑   Southwest Idaho Mountain Biking Association (SWIMBA), P.O. Box
    1443, Boise, ID 83701. Or see www.swimba.org.
❑   International Mountain Biking Association, P.O. Box 7578, Boulder,
    CO 80306. Phone: 303-545-9011. Or see www.imba.org.

MOUNTAIN BIKE RACING:
Wild Rockies Mountain Bike Race Series, P.O. Box 7075, Boise, ID 83707.
Phone: 342-3910. Website: www.wildrockies.com

EMERGENCY CONTACTS:
Ada County Search and Rescue: 911 or 846-7610.

INTERNET SITES:
❑   My site: www.idahofile.com.
❑   Idaho Travel and Tourism: www.visitid.com
❑   Idaho Department of Parks and Recreation: www.idahoparks.org
❑   Mountain Bike Review: www.mtbr.com
❑   Dirt World: www.dirtworld.com
❑   Mountain Bike magazine: www.mountainbike.com
❑   Mountain Bike Action magazine: www.mbaction.com
❑   Bike magazine: www.bikemag.com

ADVERTISING GALLERY

Please support the following businesses because they support *you!*

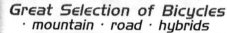